ILLINOIS · MISSOURI · KANSAS · OKLAHOMA

ROUTE 66

America's First Main Street

By SPENCER CRUMP

Zeta Publishers Company

TEXAS · NEW MEXICO · ARIZONA · CALIFORNIA

Dedicated to My Grandson
Benjamin Lewis McCarthy

ROUTE 66: America's First Main Street
By SPENCER CRUMP

Library of Congress Catalog Card No. 96:060658
ISBN (Hardcover) 0-918376-19-X
ISBN (Softcover) 0-918376-18-1

First Edition, September 1994
Second Printing, March 1995
Third Printing, August 1995

Revised Second Edition, July 1996

Published by Zeta Publishers Company
Post Office Box 38, Corona del Mar, California 92625-0038

Art Direction by Victoria Crump McCarthy

COVER: Joshua Trees formed forests along Route 66
near the Mojave Desert towns of Victorville and Barstow.

ACKNOWLEDGMENTS

The man who made the sights and sounds of Route 66 come to life was Bobby Troup, composer of *Get Your Kicks on Route 66*, and if a single person deserves credit for giving fame to America's First Main Street, it is Bobby Troup. I express my gratitude to him for permitting me to use the lyrics in this book.

The maps of Route 66 in the 1932 guide, *National Old Trails Road and U.S. Highway 66*, published by the Automobile Club of Southern California. give valuable insights into motoring at that time. The author thanks Thomas V. Kernan Jr., president of the Club; William R. Scharf, chief cartographer, and Jeffrey Wilensky of the Club's engineering and technical services, for making these maps available. Some of the book's advertisements are reproduced; please note that they refer to businesses that may no longer be in operation.

I also offer my thanks to others who have assisted me. A special word of appreciation goes to Alan R. McElwain, my boss at the time that I wrote material for magazines and newspapers when at the All-Year Club of Southern California early in my career. He taught me more about writing techniques than I could ever have learned from a thousand courses. Others on my "thank you" list are John Crump, coordinator of production; Delwin Jones, for many fine suggestions; Sally Poe of Gallup, author of *66 Sights on Route 66* and *Gallup: Six Decades of Route 66*; Teri Cleeland, chairperson of the Williams Historic Preservation Commission, and Elaine Marcinek, for technical services. I also thank Robert B. Finney of the Phillips Petroleum Company Archives, and Ruth Sigler Avery, daughter-in-law of Cyrus Stevens Avery, who envisioned the development of Route 66.

I also thank Paul Taylor, managing editor and publisher of *Route 66 Magazine*, for his encouragement and genial assistance.

In addition, I extend my appreciation to Cynthia Fink Walker for her valued assistance and encouragement.

Printed & Bound in the United States of America.

All of the joys of travelling Route 66 — " Chicago to L.A., 2,000 miles all the way" — come to life in this vintage postcard. (Lake County, Illinois, Museum/Curt Teich Postcard Archives)

Route 66 was exactly that, a route, and not an interstate or a freeway. Route 66, that fabled artery made famous in song and scenery, was actually a collection of roads tied together by highway signs. Unlike modern interstates, Route 66 frequently went directly on surface streets through cities, and, moreover, even took motorists to downtown areas in some communities. Automobiles and trucks following it halted at stop signs and signals, just as did local residents who travelled on it daily. When they left a city, drivers stepped on the gas, cruising along at 40 or 50 miles an hour, and as the "66" era was ending,

even at 65 or 70. Unlike the interstates, there were no formal "exits." One could build a ramp to a motel, service station, or other facility, even though the driveway was in the middle of the desert or in the heart of a city.

While the pavement on today's interstates is consistent, the surfaces of Old Route 66 variously changed from gravel to dirt to asphalt to brick, to concrete, and not necessarily in order, as it went through different states, counties, and cities whose preferences and budgets called for different materials.

At the time, those of us who used "66" never

thought about the deficiencies or differences.

It was the only thing we knew, and we thought it was great!

Route 66 is both something in people's fantasies and a physical road on which a motorist can still, in many places, drive in an automobile or truck, enjoying scenery and people seemingly untouched by time.

Cyrus Steven Avery was the highway official that envisioned and spurred the construction of "66" in 1926. The cult of Route 66 emerged in the 1980s and 1990s largely as the result of Bobby Troup, the artist whose 1947 song, *Get Your Kicks on Route 66*, romanticized the highway some 21 years after the route's establishment. The 1960s television series *Route 66* enhanced the fable that the song inaugurated. And of course the roadway came to life with the folks who ran mom-and-pop motels, cafes, service stations, and souvenir shops. It also did so with the men and women who cruised over the route to or from California and Illinois and told of their happy experiences.

Travelling over Route 66 was an adventure, and, at that, a very fun and educational one. There were towns and cities with diverse characters, and different kinds of buildings, terrain, bridges, climate, and other things to see and enjoy. And there were the fascinating tourist "traps" where the family could buy firecrackers, Native

This vehicle, typical of those used by the Oklahoma migrants to reach California over Route 66 in the 1930s, is at Route 66 Antiques on West Sixth Street in Amarillo. Route 66 once travelled on West Sixth.

Sparkling soon after leaving the assembly line, this 1926 roadster was one of approximately 15 million Model T's produced starting in 1908. The "T" also came in sedan and truck editions. (Ford Motor Company Collection)

Americans' blankets and pottery, ash trays, lassos, Indian, Spanish, or American dolls, and T-shirts, embellished with the name of a state, city, or tribe. One could also enjoy winding roads over mountains and alongside beaches, by caverns and lakes, and Indian reservations. And, of course, every place sold colorful picture postcards of where motorists had been for only a penny each.

Along the way, travellers could see prairie dogs, those little rodents who tunnel under the ground, peeking curiously at passing cars, and they could in the spring enjoy fields of wildflowers. Those blossoms still appear, but the prairie dogs are disappearing as farms and buildings change the landscape.

In the early twentieth century, America changed more rapidly than any time in its previous history. The reasonable prices of automobiles and their improving quality made the public demand more and better highways. The eastern part of America boasted a system of roads which was much more extensive than in the Midwest or West, thanks to it being settled earlier.

After Cyrus Steven Avery and the highway officials completed plans for what would be Route 66 (See Pages 8 & 9), they awaited for the official

5

Here is the Chicago area showing the beginning of Route 66 in 1930. (Copyright Automobile Club of Southern California; used by permission)

approval from Washington, D. C., so they could implement their plans. The big day was July 23, 1926, when Cyrus Avery received a letter from the Secretary of Interior proclaiming the birth of Route 66.

Just 23 years before, motorists made the first coast-to-coast automobile trip. The trip from San Francisco to New York required nine days, indicating the status of highways — and cars — at the time.

1926 was a very good year for America. This was midway in the era that would go down as The Roaring Twenties: The stock market boomed, encouraging even lower income people to invest; better automobiles were built; the cities grew as hotels and office buildings were erected, giving skylines to even the smaller cities. Despite Prohibition, the larger towns had speakeasies where one could buy booze; motion pictures were maturing and new theaters graced even villages; the nation was on the roll with good farm prices, and a variety of new products for consumers became part of American life.

Route 66 was born just eight years after World War I (1914-1918), and people generally had good jobs. There were such technical advancements as cross-country telephone calls, electric ice-making refrigerators, home toasters, and washing machines. Electric or gas dryers were some two decades away. The phone company was offering home service for $4 a month, but people in the 1920s accepted that one calling even locally needed to give the number orally to the operator. By the early 1930s, dials came into general use in most parts of the nation although some rural areas did not enjoy that convenience for several decades. And it took just five cents to make a local call.

The cost of phoning over a long distance was fairly expensive, with a daytime call between Chicago and L.A. costing approximately $3.00 for three minutes. That was just about a half day's pay for the average worker. Individuals and businesses used the Western Union telegraph system to send urgent messages, which cost approximately half or less than the charge for a phone call. The basic rate was for 10 words, and senders played with words to avoid paying more. The messages went from a central Western Union office in the business sections of cities or at the railroad depot in smaller towns, and then were delivered by telephone or a messenger riding a bicycle. A lower rate applied to overnight dispatches as compared to those delivered on the same day sent. Advances in telephone technology reduced the costs of long distance calls by the 1960s, and the FAX machines of the 1980s in ef-

MARSHALL FIELD & CO'S RETAIL STORE, RANDOLPH, STATE, WASHINGTON STS. AND WABASH AVENUE.

The Marshall Field department store in Chicago, shown here in the 1920s, became a bigger attraction when patrons could use Route 66 to reach it. BELOW: There was relatively little traffic on Chicago's Lake Shore Drive in the mid-1920s.

He Was Mr. Route 66

Many people worked together to plan, build, and operate Route 66, but the individual most responsible for the famous highway was Cyrus Steven Avery of Tulsa, 56 years of age when the artery was born and ahead of his time not only in advocating good roads, but also in his perception of how to develop them.

Avery (1871-1962) in effect became the "father" of Route 66.

A native of Pennsylvania, he moved as a teenager to Oklahoma when it was still Indian Territory. He grew up on a farm near Spavinaw Creek, and was graduated from William Jewell College in Missouri. He and his wife, Essie, made their home in Tulsa; their marriage lasted for 65 years and she died in 1962.

A matter that concerned many thoughtful people during the 1920s was the resurgence of the Klu Klux Klan in several cities outside the South where the organization terrorized African-Americans and other groups following the Civil War. Instead of targeting only blacks, these white-robed and masked Klansmen in the 1920s also went after Jews, Catholics, liberals, and activists of labor unions. In some cities, police officers went so far as to block off public streets where Klansmen were burning crosses.

One incident of KKK violence occurred May 31 and June 1, 1921, in Tulsa. The Klansmen burned the homes on 36 city blocks belonging to African-Americans and other minorities, murdering more than 300 people. The Red Cross and dismayed Tulsa citizens collected money for the victims. State and county authorities appointed Cyrus Avery to supervise relief for the victims and serve as treasurer of a reconstruction committee that collected money for survivors. Avery's family recalled that Klan sympathizers attempted to divert funds, but he stood firm and saw that the funds were used as intended.

Avery was nicknamed "Mr. Democrat." Friends persuaded him to campaign for governor of Oklahoma in an effort to improve conditions but he was defeated in the 1934 primary.

Meanwhile, the governor in 1924 appointed Cyrus Avery to chairman of the three-member Oklahoma State Highway Commission. The U.S. Department of Agriculture appointed him along with four representatives of other states to a special committee to devise routes and insignia for a federal highway commission.

Avery had more than an interest in good roads. The Averys soon after World War I opened the Old English Inn, which included a restaurant and gas station across from their farm at the junction of Highways 33 and 35, approximately seven miles from Tulsa.

In the 1920s, planners envisioned a route which would reach southern California by way of Missouri, Kansas, Colorado, Utah, and Nevada. Assorted cities lobbied to have the route go through their communities, knowing that the traffic would bring prosperity.

Instead of using the names of famous people or trails, the planners decided to use numbers to designate highways, a practice that has continued through the years. They also decided that east-west routes would have even numbers and north-south highways would have odd ones. In addition, the policy-makers decided to use the numeral "0" to identify major highways.

Cyrus Avery and his supporters managed to have the Chicago to Santa Monica highway moved southward to Oklahoma, Texas, New Mexico, and Arizona. Considering the alternatives, the route made sense because it avoided the heavier snows northward and also the longer stretches of deserts. Oklahoma ended up with more miles of the highway than any state along the way.

Avery's group wanted to reserve "60" as the number for this route, which all agreed would be

Cyrus Stevens Avery

a major one. Even though numbered shields and road maps were produced with the favored number, champions of other routes won the battle for the "60" application.

Undaunted, Avery and his colleagues mulled the remaining numbers. The figure that would be magic and memorable, "66" was available. The conferees concluded that it certainly would serve the purpose.

Even though it lacked the important "0," Route 66 indeed became the Main Street of America.

The intersection of State and Madison Streets in Chicago was described as the busiest corner in the world during the 1920s. BELOW: Visitors in a 1920s scene view Lincoln Park Drive. In the background is the President Grant monument.

11369

fect provided "telegram" machines in homes and offices which not only transmitted words but also images on paper.

Speaking of technology, people could buy a very neat new item, electric refrigerators. Those in the 1920s came with two small ice cube trays and a freezer compartment hardly larger than the space it took to hold them; there was also a miniscule amount of space for storing food. Electric refrigerators were expensive in relation to salaries, and therefore few middle-class homes had them. Most people relied on the insulated wooden "ice boxes," which were literally that: An insulated box into which one put blocks of ice to cool perishable food. The householder used an ice pick, which looked like a screwdriver with a point on the end, to chop chunks from the block of ice to prepare tea or cool water. Ice came by way of large trucks which got their supplies at central plants and cruised neighborhoods. The housewife received a square sign bearing the ice company's name and numbers to advise whether the family wanted to receive 25, 50, 75, or 100 pounds (usually the maximum size of a block) of ice. More and more households purchased ice-making electric refrigerators during the 1930s. With more electric refrigerators, ice companies in the 1940s began to use their facilities to store soft drinks and beer until it was distributed to stores.

Another familiar figure in the neighborhood was the milkman. While milk was available in grocery markets, some households preferred at-home delivery to save a trip to the store. Milk in paper cartons was two decades away. Milk came in various sizes, but the most popular was a one quart bottle. These bottles had a globe-type top

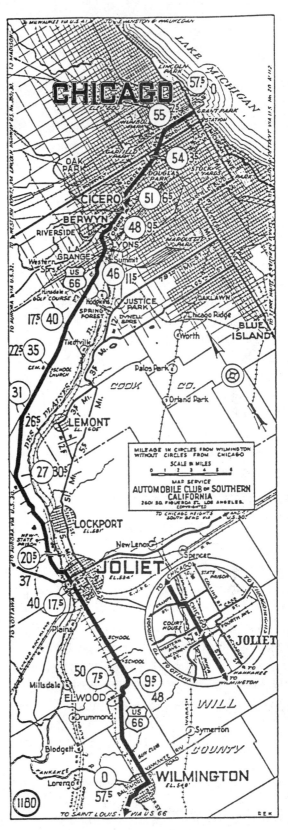

Copyright Automobile Club of Southern California; Used by Permission

The Song That Created a Legend

The man responsible, more than any other person, for elevating Route 66 to cult status is Bobby Troup, the actor-musician who wrote *Get Your Kicks on Route Sixty-six,* the folk song which reminds America of a golden era.

It's true that the highway with its bundle of attractions was there for many years before he drove over it, but Bobby Troup made it possible for people to sing about them and enjoy those attractions even more.

Born in Harrisburg, Pennsylvania, as Robert William Troup Jr., he graduated from the Wharton School of Business at the University of Pennsylvania. One of his first songs, *Daddy,* was recorded by the Sammy Kaye Orchestra, a "big band" of the 1930s and 1940s. It was No. 1 on the Hit Parade for many weeks.

Soon after completing college Bobby Troup got a job as a songwriter and arranger for Tommy Dorsey, another of the legendary band leaders of the '30s and '40s. His pay was $75 a week. After the 1941 Pearl Harbor attack, he joined the Marine Corps and served in the Pacific from 1942 to 1946.

When he returned from the service, Bobby Troup, 26 years of age at the time, could have gone to work for his family's music stores in Lancaster and Harrisburg, but he was determined to test his talent as a songwriter. He and his then-wife, Cynthia, in 1946 headed for Los Angeles in their 1941 Buick convertible. While they were dining at a restaurant on the Pennsylvania Turnpike, Cynthia Troup looked at a map and suggested that he write a song about Route 40, on which they were travelling. He discarded the idea because they were almost ready to turn onto Route 66.

As they left Saint Louis, motoring west on Route 66, she hesitantly made another suggestion for a song.

"Get your kicks on Route 66," she said.

"God, what a marvelous idea for a song!" Bobby Troup replied. "What a great title!"

Checking maps, he determined that the distance from Chicago to L.A. was "more than two thousand miles all the way."

As they continued west, he began to put the song together. The lyrics were a virtual "map" of Route 66.

Driving over the highway, the Troups enjoyed the things that made up Route 66, ranging from the pleasures of the Meramec Caverns and the Will Rogers Memorial to the ordeals of a snowstorm in Amarillo and the heat of the desert.

Once in Los Angeles, he managed to meet Nat "King" Cole and play some of his songs for him. After doing so, he told the great singer that he was writing a new song, and Cole agreed to hear it. Nat Cole loved it, Bobby Troup said, and decided to record it.

Get Your Kicks on Route Sixty-six was an immediate hit, and over the years it became an American classic. When he would meet "King" Cole years later, Bobby Troup recalled, the singer would tell him that of all the musical selections he presented, the requests for Route 66 topped them all.

Over the years, countless singers and musical groups made records of *Get Your Kicks on Route Sixty-six.*

That single song established Troup in the entertainment world. He went on to write other songs and appear as an singer, pianist, and an actor. A multi-talented individual, he made eight record albums. He and his present wife, actress, Julie London, appeared as the doctor and nurse respectively in the popular television series Emergency.

One disappointment for Bobby Troup was the fact that the television series *Route 66* did not use his music as a theme. Instead they contracted for Nelson Riddle to compose the music which, Troup assumes, avoided paying him royalties.

When one motors across Route 66 even in the 1990s, *Get Your Kicks on Route Sixty-six* frequently comes over the radio, making the trip even more pleasant.

Reference to "66" in books and on postcards prior to Bobby Troup's famous song referred to the artery as a "highway." When the song became a part of Americana, the references changed to "route."

Many artists have made recordings of *Get Your Kicks on Route Sixty-six*. Besides Bobby Troup and Nat King Cole, they include Nat's daughter, Natalie Cole; Bing Crosby, the Andrews Sisters, Perry Como, George Maharis, Paul Anka, Chuck Berry, Michael Martin Murphey, Sammy Davis Jr., The Rolling Stones, and Earthquake.

And the list goes on.

Bobby Troup once said he thought he was writing about a highway, not a legend. Actually Bobby Troup helped make Route 66 the legend that it is.

Here are the lyrics:

Bobby Troup

Get Your Kicks on Route Sixty-six!

If you ever plan to motor West
Travel my way, take the highway that's
the best.
Get your Kicks on Route Sixty-six!
It winds from Chicago to L.A.,
More than two thousand miles all the way.
Get your Kicks on Route Sixty-six!
Now you go thru Saint Looey and Joplin,
Missouri

And Oklahoma City is mighty pretty;
You'll see Amarillo; Gallop, New Mexico;
Flagstaff, Arizona; Don't forget Winona,
Kingman, Barstow, San Bernardino.
Won't you get hip to this timely tip:
When you make that California trip
Get Your Kicks on Route Sixty-six!

Words & Music by Bobby Troup; Copyright Londontown Music, ASCAP; used by permission.

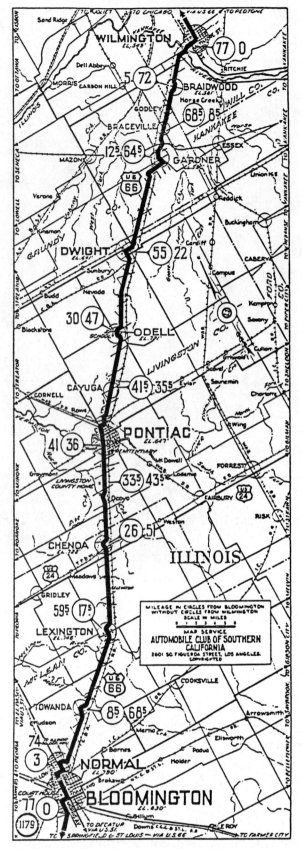

displaying the cream, which was not generally mixed into the milk itself until the 1940s. Despite the fact that the automobile and truck had arrived, many milkmen made their rounds in a van pulled by a horse even into the early 1930s.

Two other conveniences served the housewife. One was the Fuller Brush Man, who went from door-to-door in neighborhoods with a suitcase carrying the usual brushes, and a few new ones, for cleaning. He gained entry to a home by presenting a small brush as a gift, and then demonstrated other brushes which would be handy. The other direct salesman was the Watkins representative. He offered spices and flavorings, some of which were not available at the time in grocery stores.

After receiving an order, the salesman would return in a few days with the products ordered. There were lesser-known firms which offered similar products, but Fuller and Watkins dominated the field until the 1950s, when door-to-door sales plummeted with the proliferation of shopping malls, larger grocery stores, and specialty shops. Some representatives earned commissions which were high enough to put their pay substantially ahead of other wage earners.

By way of explanation, the male gender is used to describe these sales representatives because few women took such jobs, either by choice or availability. Women, even those with educations superior to men, in general found it extremely difficult to obtain the jobs or promotions for which they were qualified until the feminist movement that started in the late 1960s.

The big item of these times was the automobile, which in the 1920s came into its own as a vehicle that could unleash people and take them to new horizons without being captive to the schedules of a train, trolley, or bus. Without having to wait for public transportation schedules, it was always ready for a casual cruise to nearby points of interest which previously were inaccessible because of time or distance. And automobiles were in the financial reach of a growing number of families.

The average annual wage in America at the time was approximately $1,200, $100 monthly. A big break-through came in the teens when auto maker Henry Ford (1863-1947) began paying assembly-line workers $5 a day, an unheard-of wage for the time. This gave them approximately $1,500 a year, well above the average. It was not uncommon for wage earners in the higher brackets to make $5,000 or more a year, and doctors, dentists, lawyers, and other professionals made much more, but few received the pay that was prevalent in the late 20th century. Women, however, generally received much lower pay than their male counterparts. Affirmative hiring and equal opportunity laws were decades away, as was the feminist movement. The type of executives of large companies who now receive upwards of a million dollars annually felt they were doing well to take home $100,000 a year before income taxes. Wage earners could buy a loaf of bread for 9 cents, a new Model T Ford cost as little as $400, gasoline was 10 cents a gallon, and the price of a decent middle-class home for $1,000 to $8,000. In smaller towns, some very good houses sold for as little as $400.

Many families survived on considerably less than the average wage. Gas, water, and electric bills seldom totalled more than $1 a month. This was the glorious era typified in Sinclair Lewis' *Main Street* and *Babbitt*, those novels that painted the way that life of mid-America was in the 1920s. Few women followed careers for two reasons: First, because their husband's wages allowed them to remain at home with the children or be able to enjoy social clubs, and second, the "system" favored men in job assignments and promotions. The divorce rate in America was much lower in those times, and was more of a stigma than it became in the 1950s. Many women

A 1933 view shows Chicago's busy Michigan Avenue. BELOW: Meramec Caverns in Missouri advertised up and down Route 66 by painting barns to attract visitors. (Photograph by the Author)

15

ABRAHAM
LINCOLN'S
OLD HOME,
SPRINGFIELD,
ILLINOIS

Springfield, Illinois, is Abraham Lincoln country. This was Lincoln's home, in Old Route 66 days and still an attraction for visitors.

did not want to leave the security of a marriage, nor did men want to risk the possibility of high alimony payments. Most cities had women's organizations such as the Junior League, Ebell Club, or Woman's City Club. These groups had varying levels of prestige. Members attended weekly meetings where they heard lectures or played bridge and other games. The club members justified their existence by supporting charitable works for children, poor people, and those that were ill and lacked relatives or friends. Some groups operated thrift shops that provided clothing or money for the needy, and others financed additions or services at hospitals, camps for needy children, or supervised clubs for youngsters who otherwise might have been neglected. These groups were designed for damsels who were financially empowered, and not for the woman of average means. The meetings were a forum where women could display their new fur

pieces or other luxurious items of apparel and discuss their husbands' business or professional practices. The city's newspaper customarily assigned women reporters to cover the meetings and write stories about them, knowing that the articles would dazzle envious non-members who aspired to join a club. These stories embellished the "society" pages, which also included news of engagements or weddings among the socially prominent. As the years moved on, newspapers changed these pages into sections for all women and then to ones for families. In the 1990s, with more women pursuing careers, even the once exclusive clubs found it difficult to recruit members.

These upper-income women also found no problems, financially at least, in operating their households. The pay for cleaning or kitchen services was negotiable and there were no minimum wage laws.

In the era from the 1920s to 1950s, there was

less division between various groups of people that made up America than those fragmentations that began in 1945 after World War II, although there were faint sounds that it was splintering. Society became more stratified starting in the 1960s. Even then, the owners of factories or department stores were the ones who resided in larger houses in more "exclusive" sections of towns, while doctors, lawyers, and other professionals resided in the same neighborhoods as their patients or clients. People could have the friendly family doctor make house calls at almost any hour and charge only moderate fees; this continued until the late 1940s and early 1950s. The great majority of people — the office managers, store owners or executives, and craftsmen — managed to achieve their goals of decent incomes for their families by holding only a high school diploma, something with which they could be proud because many individuals dropped out of school in the eighth or ninth grades. In the late twentieth century, enrolling in a high school and attending classes fairly regularly would result in the scholar receiving a diploma in most public schools, even though he or she might be delinquent in some basic skills. In the first half of the century, however, a student actually had to demonstrate that there had been a reasonable amount of learning the subject manner. If the student did not, it meant repeating courses until he or she earned a satisfactory grade. Parents, students, and employers accepted this system as a reasonable one because it reflected standards. Over the years, parents changed from accepting the grades assigned for a child's performance in schools to pushing teachers to assign "A" almost indiscriminately or lose the community's support with taxes. In many senses, a high school diploma earned before the 1950s was the equivalent, at least from the standpoints of skill, to a bachelor's degree thereafter.

Four-year college degrees in the 1920s through

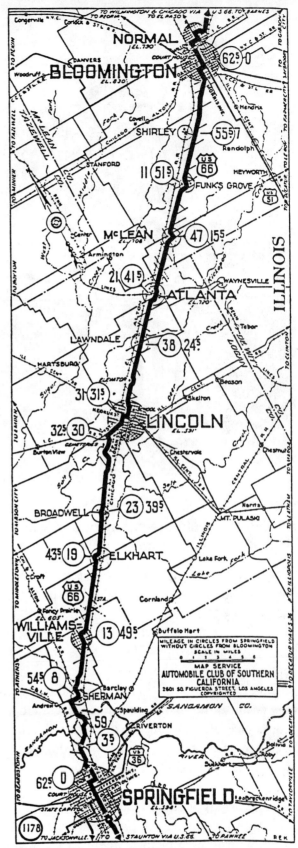

17

Built in 1848, this mansion in Bloomington was the home of David Davis, a judge before whom Abraham Lincoln practiced law and who later was a U.S. Supreme Court justice. The mansion is open to the public. (Courtesy Bloomington-Normal Area Convention and Visitors Bureau)

1950s indeed were prized, for very few young men or women had the financial backing or willingness to continue beyond high school in a society where the importance of higher education had not yet trickled past the families where members had degrees. The men fortunate enough to earn college degrees found better-than-average jobs because the market was not yet glutted with people gleefully holding up diplomas. A relatively few women earned professional degrees, and those who received them in medicine or dentistry often found that they had to specialize in treating children. Many women who attended colleges or universities frequently did so because the educational environment enabled them to meet young men with upward mobility who wanted educated

wives that might help them achieve their goals. In order to deal fairly with women, we must recognize that most of them prized knowledge and were ambitious. The social structure of the day failed to extend job opportunities to qualified women, and many resented the situation. In that era, unfortunately, there was no feminist movement or other support for those who wanted careers and there were no organizations that could effectively help them protest their lots in life. There were no equal opportunity laws any more than there was legislation establishing minimum wages or hours in a work week.

The situation for African-Americans was a desperate one. In some places there was outright segregation and subtle racism in almost all areas.

While a handful of blacks achieved economic and social success, most of them suffered as second-class citizens despite Americans' expressions of pride for freedom.

In regard to cars, the modestly-priced Model T was affordable to many people and soon after its 1908 introduction became famous as an automotive workhorse. It was available as a two-seater, sedan, or in various truck models. About the time that Route 66 was born, approximately 15 million copies of the vehicle had been sold — but America's love affair with the Model T was waning. This auto required cranking because it lacked the self-starter that other cars offered as standard in the 1920s. Once the Model T's engine chucked away, however, it would take families to town and on trips into the country. General Motors Corporation, founded in 1916 by William Durant (1861-1947) and Louis Chevrolet (1879-1941), began offering a wider variety of automobiles. It introduced the Chevrolet, which in the 1920s became popular with motorists. In 1928 Ford introduced the famous Model A, a low-priced auto which incorporated refinements already offered by competitors; it eventually became a collector's item.

For the buyer willing to spend the whopping sum of a thousand dollars for an automobile, he or she could select from a wide choice of cars, including Auburns, Buicks, Cadillacs, Chryslers, Dodges, Hupmobiles, Hudsons, Nashes, or Willys-Knights. Packards also were popular cars and came in three sizes and prices ranges, all of which were a cut above most other autos and inspired a saying popular at the time, "It runs like a Packard," in reference to any piece of well-crafted machinery. Another well-liked automobile was the Studebaker, which named its models the Champion, the smallest of the line; the Commander, a medium-sized vehicle, and the President, its largest offering. American-built cars dominated the streets. The few imports on

Among the tributes to Lincoln in Springfield is this statue.

American roads included the upscale Rolls Royces, and Mercedes, which indeed attracted attention because of their style and sizes, plus the onlooker's awareness that only rich people could afford them. A few diminutive British Austins

19

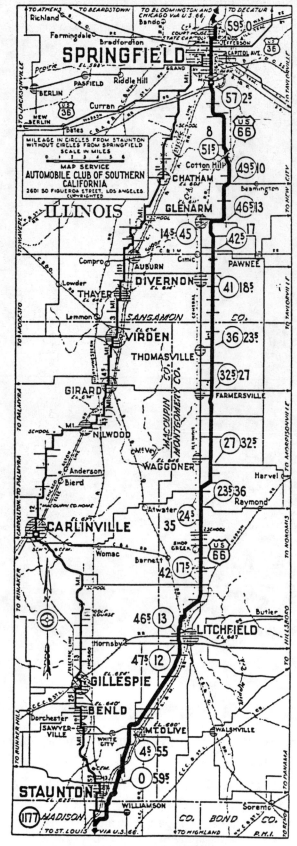

made their way to America, but Yanks disdained them because they lacked the power or roominess to provide comfort, particularly for long-distance driving and over the rough terrain that they would find in parts of Route 66.

Buying an automobile in the 1920s was a different experience than in the 1960s and beyond. There were no auto malls, and few purchasers ventured away from their home towns. Why? Virtually all dealers sold their cars at list prices, with buyers excepting this policy. The the only cushion for a better deal was in the trade-in allowance, which in those times was very much the same regardless of where one dealt.

In the 1920s and early 1930s, there were no automatic transmissions, and only the larger and more expensive cars had trunks. Spare tires for the smaller cars were mounted on the back of the vehicle, whereby some of the larger autos boasted two spares that were carried in "well" indentations on each of the front fenders. Almost every car and truck had "running boards," which spanned a space of eight to ten inches outside the vehicle's door. They were used to help motorists enter the automobiles, or, as can be noted in old motion pictures, as places for the police or gangsters to stand while the vehicle chased and shot at other cars.

Trunks were added to automobiles in the late 1920s and early 1930s, although a few of the more expensive cars had them earlier. Running boards disappeared in approximately 1941 with model changes which made wider and roomier interiors and were lower to facilitate entry. At about the same time, divided front windshields disappeared in favor of a wider one-piece windows that gave a better view and embellished cars with a more streamlined look.

As explained earlier, not only did the mid-1920s bring about Route 66, but these years also were the ones when radio broadcasting grew rapidly. Quality of programming varied according

20

The Ford Model A, introduced in 1928, became a collector's item. This is the automobile's offering for 1931, the last year of production for the Model A. (Ford Motor Company Collection)

to the size of a station's audience or market size, but listeners generally heard music, either recorded or live depending on the stations' budgets. They also enjoyed locally-written drama and comedy shows, plus a smattering of news gleaned from newspapers. Listeners had a limited number of radio stations from which to choose. Only a few rural towns had a station, and even in metropolitan cities such as Los Angeles or Chicago there were only nine or ten broadcasters. FM stations did not arrive until after World War II. Television was a science-fiction "dream," touched occasionally in fantasy motion pictures until it arrived in homes during the late 1940s. In

the 1930s, radio networks began to thrive and develop "stars" of musical programs and other presentations. The major networks were the National Broadcasting Company, which in major cities had both the "blue" and "red" networks, and the Columbia Broadcasting Company, at the onset a weak second in the race for audiences. Fairness laws forced NBC to sell its "red" network, which eventually emerged as the American Broadcasting

21

Youth is served, splendidly, powerfully, pridefully and yet economically, by this charming new 1927 Buick. It is princely in its luxury and grace of line, and it has the year's most important contribution to the pleasure of motoring—an engine, *vibrationless beyond belief*

THE GREATEST BUICK EVER BUILT

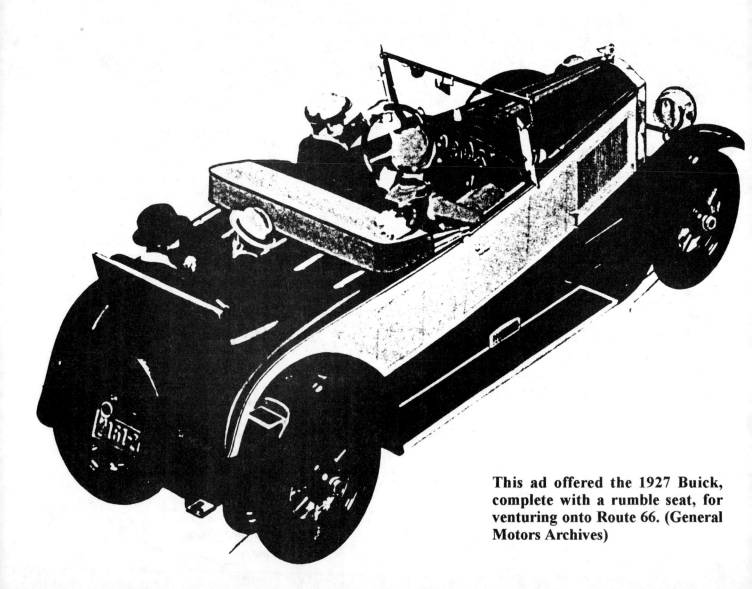

This ad offered the 1927 Buick, complete with a rumble seat, for venturing onto Route 66. (General Motors Archives)

Autos Made Route 66

A Corvette similar to the one used in the *Route 66* television series posed for this photograph in front of Ron Chavez's Club Cafe in Santa Rosa, New Mexico. (Courtesy of *Route 66 Magazine*)

Automobiles were the name of the game in the 1920s and the inspiration for the creation of Route 66. Over that two-lane highway which in 1926 took off for California, automobiles of many names and descriptions rolled across America.

America's prosperity in the early twentieth century was largely fueled by the automobile, that wondrous invention that opened the countryside for jaunts. Cars also made it easy to travel to cities without worrying about train schedules or the cost of tickets for family members, who rode free in an automobile. The Dow Jones Industrial Average is a Wall Street thermometer of 30 representative stocks which measures the ups and downs of stocks in general. In the 1920s, however, it was composed of just 20 stocks. When The Wall Street Journal, which determines how the averages are calculated, decided in 1928 to increase the number of stocks in the scale to 30, they used the auto industry for 40 percent of the 10 additions: the manufacturers Chrysler and

Nash, along with Bethlehem Steel Corporation, which supplied steel for the auto makers, and the Texas Corporation, a producer of gasoline for cars. Driving automobiles was a pleasure in the 1920s, according to those who ventured onto the roads during those years. Families and couples enjoyed Sunday jaunts into the countryside, often stopping at a recommended restaurant for lunch. With Route 66 constructed, longer trips were possible.

Driving laws and courtesies were followed more carefully in the early days of motoring than in the era that followed the close of Route 66. If a car was moving slowly in the left lane of a four-lane highway, a simple "honk" reminded the motorist to pull to the right and he or she did so without feeling offended, whereas many modern drivers would take offense at such an act. At night, a "blink" of the headlights from the rear accomplished the same thing.

Drivers in most areas stopped for stop signs and

A dealer's 1931 classified advertisement showed the prices for various automobiles offered for sale at this time.

for pedestrians as soon as they put a foot off the curb. Few motorists wove in and out of traffic to demonstrate their pride in powerful automobiles and at the same time gain a few seconds.

Almost every area, particularly metropolitan ones, along Old Route 66 have experienced immense increases in population. More automobiles, and more powerful ones at that, have made driving for pleasure a nightmare.

Did the author have any cars that became classics or semi-classics? Yes, four such automobiles, although all of them were not purchased new. They were a 1936 Ford coupe (no rear seats), a 1940 Ford sedan, a 1948 Studebaker, and a 1957 Chevrolet (with the ornate fins).

All of his cars were fun.

The earlier automobiles came equipped with running boards to make it easy for passengers entering and alighting from cars; these were eliminated in 1940. In the 1920s and 1930s, the motorist who selected a coupe had the choice of a rumble-seat, where two passengers could ride in the open-air where the trunk belonged, or a trunk and no rumble seat. The refinement of the club coupe gave what in effect was an enclosed rumble-seat. These gave way in the late 1940s to the two-door sedan, which really existed for years.

Automatic gear shifts arrived as an option on higher-priced automobiles in the late 1930s. Air conditioners came as an option in the late 1950s.

Here are a few words on the listings. Because there were no foreign-built cars that made it to America in commercial quantities, the list includes only U.S. products. Also, comic Jack Benny's fabled Maxwell (there really was such an automobile) does not make the roster because only those companies that operated during the Route 66 years of 1926 to 1984 are noted. (Production of the Maxwell ceased in 1924.)

By the way, negotiating the price of an automobile was a different experience until the late 1940s. The dealer's list price of a car was very close to what you paid, with the only difference coming in the allowance for a trade-in vehicle. Selling automobiles therefore could be a lucrative business. The dealer was protected by having a territory in which there was virtually no competition, at least for the brand he sold. Salesmen seldom resorted to high pressure methods or discussions over discounts, and many remained with a dealer for years.

Few customers, therefore, ventured beyond their own home towns to make deals.

One joy of purchasing an automobile in the 1930s until the early 1960s was the option of travelling to the factory to get the car. Prices during those years

ARROYO SECO BRIDGE. PASADENA, CALIFORNIA.

The countryside was almost completely undeveloped when this picture of Pasadena's Arroyo Seco (Dry Wash) Bridge was made in the 1920s.

included a delivery fee, and one could save it by arranging to pick up the new automobile where it was built, usually Detroit but possibly Cleveland, Kenosha, South Bend, or some other factory town. Saving the fee gave the buyer enough money to take the family to the city where the automobile was manufactured, with change leftover for gasoline, motels, and meals. It was a break-even situation but one that provided a low-cost vacation, with the return over Route 66 if one resided in the West.

Because public transportation was cheap (usually 5 cents per ride in a city) and plentiful by bus or trolley, one automobile per family was enough for most families except the most affluent ones. Houses typically were built with a single-car garage until the late 1940s when the family owning two or three cars came into being.

In 1930, just after the stock market crash but before its impact on consumers, Americans could choose from no less than 40 brands of passenger cars produced by American manufacturers. The Depression of the 1930s wiped out most of these companies, and the competitive pressures on the automotive industry following World War II caused all but three manufacturers (Chrysler, Ford, General Motors) to close.

Here is a list of the major American automobile builders, with the initial year of production and the final year appearing last):

American Austin (1930 - 1934) was established in 1930 at Butler, Pennsylvania, by 21-year-old Roy Evans who envisioned a market of small-car devotees. Its maximum speed was 50 miles an hour. The list price was $435, but many contemporary full-sized cars sold for less, making that automobile unattractive for the average buyer, and the company closed after four years. The little cars made a humorous appearance in the 1931 motion picture *A Connecticut Yankee* starring Will Rogers, Myrna Loy, and Maureen O'Sullivan. In the film Rogers dreams he is back in King Arthur's Court, and when he meets trouble he is rescued by people driving a

long line of the small autos up to the royal castle. The company should not be confused with British Austin, which has produced automobiles of many sizes, including small ones.

American Bantam Car Company (1937 - 1941) produced a revived and restyled version of American Austin. Based in Butler, Pennsylvania, it built not only conventional passenger cars but also station wagons and small trucks in miniature designs. The company designed the Jeep in 1940 for the U. S. Army but was unable to mass-produce the vehicles. It went out of business in 1941.

American Motors Corporation (1954 - 1961) was formed when Nash acquired the struggling *Hudson Motor Car Company*. The new firm discontinued using the Hudson name in 1957 and concentrated on producing the Rambler, a compact car introduced by Nash in 1950 and built at its plant in Kenosha, Wisconsin. The company also marketed the diminutive Metropolitan, unveiled in 1954 and built for the firm by Austin of England.

Auburn Automobile Company (1900 - 1937) was formed in Auburn, Indiana, by brothers Frank and Morris Eckhart whose father owned a carriage company. The firm built autos which were upscale in power and styling. It also constructed the Duesenberg and Cord. Even the energetic Errett [correct spelling] Cord, who joined Auburn in 1924 and eventually became president, could not salvage the firm when the Depression of the 1930s came.

Blackhawk, (1929 - 1930) was a lower-priced version of the famous Stutz.

Bricklin (1974 - 1976) took its name from its developer, Malcolm Bricklin, whose plant was at St. Johns, New Foundland. The automobile resembled the *DeLorean* and was intended for fans of the *Corvette*.

Buick (1903 -) was established in 1903 at Flint, Michigan, by David Buick, inventor of the enamelled bathtub. William Crapo Durant took over from Buick in 1908, using the firm as part of the foundation for his *General Motors*.

Cadillac, (1902 -) founded as the Henry Ford

Company, took a new name when Ford left a few months after its inception to establish the *Ford Motor Company*. The new name honored Antoine de la Mothe Cadillac, who founded what became America's automobile capitol, Detroit. *Cadillac* became part of *General Motors* in 1909.

Chandler, (1913 - 1929) regarded as one of the better automobiles of its era, was built in Cleveland until 1929, when it was acquired by *Hupmobile*.

Checker Cab Company (1923 - 1982) of Kalamazoo, Michigan, built sturdy taxicabs, many of which were appropriately used in the rough-and-tumble traffic of New York City. In the early 1960s it unsuccessfully attempted to market adaptations of the cabs as passenger cars to the general public.

Chevrolet (1911 -) was established by William C. Durant, who had lost control of *General Motors*, and Louis Chevrolet, a racing driver. Chevrolet soon resigned from the company. So successful was the car that Durant was able to trade his shares in the firm for ones in *General Motors*, thus regaining control of *GM* (although he lost control for the second and last time in 1920). By the 1920s, *Chevrolet* was the largest selling auto in America.

Chrysler, (1924 -) headquartered in Detroit, was formed by Walter Chrysler who had worked for *Buick* and *Willys*. He acquired Maxwell-Chalmers Motors in 1924 and the company's first entry was the upscale *Chrysler*. The company in 1928 acquired *Dodge Motors*. In that same year, the firm introduced the *Plymouth*, a smaller car, and the larger *DeSoto*, slightly cheaper than the Chrysler. After only four years, *Chrysler* achieved the No. 3 place in American automobile sales. In 1987 *Chrysler* purchased *American Motors Corporation* and with it acquired *Jeep*.

Cord (1929 - 1937) was named for Errett Cord (1894 - 1974), the head of *Auburn*, which built and marketed the car. It was priced at $3,000 — slightly more than six times the cost of the ordinary American automobile at the time. The introduction coincided with the start of the Depression, which made it difficult to market an expensive car. A 1937

A Route 66 car dealer advertised the diminutive Crosley along with the Willys and Jeep in this 1948 advertisement.

Cord offered radical lines which in beauty approached or even exceeded those of modern automobiles. Few of these cars were produced because of its price, approximately 10 times that of its contemporaries.

Corvair, (1960 - 1969) marketed under the *Chevrolet* banner, was a sporty and innovative automobile with its engine in the rear. Consumer advocate Ralph Nader attacked it in his 1965 book *Unsafe at Any Speed*, charging the car was dangerous to drive. Sales fell and its manufacturer, *General Motors*, discontinued production. The automobiles are now prized by collectors.

Corvette (1953 -) produced by *GM* and marketed under the *Chevrolet* banner, was the sports car which the main characters used in the *Route 66* television series. The show helped the automobile's sales so much that *GM* made new models available each year to the producers to keep it in the public eyes.

Crosley (1939 - 1952) was a tiny automobile built

in Marion, Indiana, by Powell Crosley, a pioneer radio manufacturer who also produced electric refrigerators.

DeLorean, (1979 - 1982) while built in Ireland, is regarded as an American product because its developer, John DeLorean, was from the United States and intended to market the automobile primarily in America.

DeSoto (1928 - 1960) was introduced to secure a marketing niche for an automobile slightly lower in price than the quality *Chrysler*.

Detroit Electric (1907 - 1938) Built in Detroit, these cars continued in production long after their era ended because of sales to a dedicated clientele. Maximum speed: 25 miles an hour. For some models, the driver sat in the back seat and steered with a tiller-like handle.

Diana (1925 - 1928) Built in St. Louis by the *Moon Motor Car Company*, this automobile cost from $1,600 to $2,900.

Doble, (1924 - 1932) was a steam-powered automobile built by Abner Doble in Emeryville, California. It could go 1,500 miles on 24 gallons of water.

Dodge (1914 -) of Detroit was formed by the Dodge brothers, who began by building engines and transmissions, and by the early 1920s was becoming a major automobile manufacturer. Chrysler acquired it in 1927.

Duesenberg (1920 - 1937) of Indianapolis was established by August and Fred Duesenberg. Specializing in luxurious automobiles, its products were driven by such luminaries as Mae West, Greta Garbo, William Randolph Hearst, and Clark Gable. It became part *Auburn Motor Car Company* in 1926.

DuPont (1920 - 1932) established at Moore, Pennsylvania, by E. Paul DuPont, an heir to the Dupont fortune. It produced a limited number of automobiles, all of them in the luxury class.

Edsel (1958 - 1960) was named for Henry Ford's son Edsel (the father of Henry Ford II) to fill a perceived marketing gap between *Ford Motor Company's* popular *Mercury* and *Lincoln* products. Despite intense merchandising, the car never attracted the buyers expected and Ford lost millions.

Essex (1918 - 1932) was part of the *Hudson Motor Car* Company in Detroit.

Ford Motor Company (1903 -) was established by Henry Ford, a young farmer's son who first wanted to invent a machine which would make farm work easier and then sought to build autos within the financial reach of the average person. His famous Model T, introduced in 1908, sold so well that by the time the car was discontinued in 1927 it represented one-half the automobiles in the world. In 1920 Ford acquired *Lincoln*, which became its entry in the luxury car category, and in 1938 introduced the *Mercury*, designed to fill the marketplace between the *Ford* and *Lincoln*. In 1958 it launched the ill-fated *Edsel* with the misconceived idea that it could fill a marketing niche just below the Lincoln.

Franklin (1902 - 1934) Situated in Syracuse, N.Y., and founded by H.H. Franklin, the company achieved fame by building air-cooled cars. Several noted aviators, among them Amelia Earhart, Charles Lindbergh, and Orville Wright, owned the cars.

Frazer (1946 - 1952) was a luxury car built by *Kaiser-Frazer* and named for Joseph Frazer, president of *K-F* and formerly the head of *Graham-Paige*.

General Motors (1908 -) formed a family of automobiles starting with existing companies and expanding with new divisions. Its cars have included *Buick, Cadillac, Chevrolet, Corvair, Corvette, Durant, Oldsmobile, LaSalle, Oakland, Oldsmobile*, and *Pontiac*. The firm was founded by William C. Durant, who lost control of the firm in 1920. He was succeeded by Alfred P. Sloan Jr., president from 1923 to 1937 and chairman of the board from 1937 to 1956. It was Sloan who pioneered annual model changes designed to cajole buyers into changing automobiles more often. In 1986, the year that Route 66 ended, *GM* introduced the *Saturn*, regarded as many as a more direct competitor to popular Japanese imports. *GM* in 1912 spearheaded the use of the engine self-starter, as opposed to the crank, a convenience found in production-line automobiles years later.

Graham-Paige (1928 - 1940) was established when brothers Joseph, Ray, and Robert Graham acquired Paige-Detroit. One of the 10 largest automobile manufacturers at the time, its share of the market declined over the years.

Hudson (1909 - 1957) of Detroit took its name from its founder, the city's department store magnate, J.L. Hudson. In 1918 the company introduced the *Essex* (1918-1932), a relatively cheap two-door sedan. It was later replaced by the *Hudson Terraplane*. Faced with financial problems in the competitive 1950s, *Hudson* merged with *Nash Motor Cars* in 1954, forming *American Motors Company*, which produced *Hudson* cars until 1957.

Hupmobile (1908 - 1940) Named for co-founder Robert Hupp, the Detroit firm produced a car designed to compete with the Ford Model T. Hupp resigned from the company in 1911. After acquiring *Chandler Cars* in 1929, the firm produced its lower-priced automobiles at that company's facility in Cleveland.

Jeep (1940 -) is an automobile brand name which has been through several ownerships. Although the vehicle was developed by *American Bantam*, that company lacked the facilities for mass production so that task was taken over by *Willys*. It proved to be a formidable tool in World War II. The name which became part of the American lexicon was inspired by the initials "G.P.," the military abbreviation for "general purpose." The little vehicle could go 60 miles an hour, climb 60 percent grades, and cross shallow rivers. When *Chrysler* purchased *America Motors Corporation* in 1987 and thereby acquired Jeep, it was able to develop variations of the little car and market them so that they contributed substantial profits.

Jordan (1916 - 1931) Based in Cleveland, this auto maker was established by Edward Jordan, a former journalist.

This advertisement hailed the power and beauty of the 1931 Willys Six, offered at reasonable price for the era.

Kaiser-Frazer (1946 - 1955) was organized by shipbuilder Henry J. Kaiser and Joseph Frazer, former head of *Graham-Paige*. Their plant was constructed during World War II by *Ford Motor Company* at Willow Run, Michigan, to build bombers for the Air Force. The products included the *Frazer*, (1946 - 1952) an upscale vehicle and the *Kaiser*, a medium-sized car In 1951 the company introduced the *Henry J*, a smaller economy auto. The *Frazer* line was discontinued in 1952 and *Henry J* production ended in 1953 at which time the company merged with *Willys-American*, which had been building *Jeeps*. In 1963 the firm changed its name to *Kaiser-Jeep*.

Kaiser-Jeep (1963 - 1970) formed in 1963 through a change of name, was acquired in 1970 by American Motors Corporation.

LaSalle (1927 - 1960) was created by *General Motors* as a lower-priced vehicle for motorists who liked Cadillacs. Production ended because the automobile lost appeal by sharing bodies with Buick and Oldsmobile.

Lincoln (1920 -) was established at Detroit by Henry Leland and soon encountered financial problems. The *Ford Motor Company* acquired the firm and used the name to identify its larger automobiles.

Marmon (1902 - 1933) of Indianapolis successfully built automobiles for a clientele preferring larger cars. Sales deteriorated over the years, and the Depression doomed the company.

Mercury (1938 -) was introduced by the Ford Motor Company to provide a product for the markets between Ford and Lincoln offerings.

Nash (1917 - 1957) of Kenosha, Wisconsin, was established by Charles Nash, former president (1912 - 1916) of General Motors. In 1954 *Nash* acquired *Hudson Motors*, and the merger created *American Motors Corporation*.

Oakland (1907 - 1932) joined the *General Motors* family in 1909. Although a popular automobile, its sales declined after *GM* in 1926 introduced the *Pontiac*, designed as a lower priced version of the car.

Oldsmobile (1901-) of Detroit originally was a one-cylinder automobile designed by Ransom Olds. The company became part of *General Motors* in 1908.

Packard (1899 - 1958) soon became a hallmark of luxury automobiles. In the mid-1930s the company introduced smaller models, although they were priced above the basic models of other manufacturers. The luxury editions were its best known models. In 1954 *Packard* merged with

Studebaker, forming *Studebaker-Packard Corporation*.

Paige-Detroit (1908 - 1927) built one of America's first moving assembly lines in its Detroit plant and was noted for producing handsome automobiles. It was acquired in 1927 by the Graham brothers who merged it into the *Graham-Paige Company*.

Peerless Motor Car Company (1900 - 1931) of Cleveland was a manufacturer of quality bicycles when it turned to producing automobiles. Its distinguished cars came with numerous engineering advances. Sales dropped hopelessly during the Depression of the 1930s, forcing it to close.

Pierce-Arrow (1901 - 1938) of Buffalo was organized by George Pierce and built prestigious automobiles, and its early 1930s models featured bodies that paralleled the designs of modern cars. Stockholders sold the company in the late 1920s to Studebaker, but when sales sagged a group of Buffalo investors repurchased the firm. The Depression of the 1930s caused to firm to close.

Plymouth (1928 -) Introduced by Chrysler to attract buyers in the low-priced field, the car offered engineering innovations and quality which soon made it the No. 3 selling automobile after *Chevrolet* and *Ford*.

Pontiac (1926 -) was launched by *General Motors* as a lower-priced version of its *Oakland*. The new automobile competed so fiercely that the older car was discontinued in 1931.

Rambler (1950 - 1970) was the name Nash selected when it introduced a compact automobile which soon became one of America's best selling cars. The name had been used for a auto produced by an early 1900s predecessor. When Nash merged into American Motors Corporation in 1954 the new firm named all of its cars Rambler.

The Edsel was an exciting automobile, as this illustration indicates, but despite aggressive marketing the automobile never turned-on the public.

They'll know you've *arrived*

when you drive up in an Edsel

Step into the 1958 Edsel and you'll soon find out where the excitement is this year.

Drivers coming toward you spot that classic vertical grille a block away. And as you pass, they glance into their rear-view mirrors for another look at this year's most exciting car.

On the open road, your Edsel is watched eagerly for the already-famous performance of its big, new V-8 Edsel Engine.

And parked in front of your home, your Edsel gets even more attention—because it always says a lot about you. It says you chose elegant styling, luxurious comfort and such exclusive features as Edsel's famous Teletouch Drive—only shift that puts the buttons where they belong, on the steering-wheel hub.

Your Edsel also means you made a wonderful buy. For of all medium-priced cars, this one really new car is actually priced the lowest.* See your Edsel Dealer this week.

*Based on actual comparison of suggested retail delivered prices of the Edsel Ranger and similarly equipped cars in the medium-price field.

EDSEL DIVISION • FORD MOTOR COMPANY

Above: Edsel Citation 2-door Hardtop. Engine: the E-475, with 10.5 to one compression ratio, 345 hp, 475 ft.-lb. torque. Transmission: Automatic with Teletouch Drive. Suspension: Ball-joint with optional air suspension. Brakes: self-adjusting.

1958 EDSEL

Of all medium-priced cars, the one that's really new is the lowest-priced, too!

Reo (1904 - 1936) was headed by Ransom Olds, who retired from Oldsmobile in 1904. Headquartered in Lansing, Michigan, the company built well engineered quality cars. In 1936, the company stopped making automobiles and produced trucks, which unlike cars sold well during the Depression. As for Olds, he lived until 1950 when he died at 86 years of age.

Rickenbacker (1922 - 1930) took its name from Captain Eddie Rickenbacker, the World War I ace. Rickenbacker's cars offered numerous engineering improvements but the company encountered financial problems.

Roamer (1916 - 1930) Situated at Kalamazoo, Michigan, and formed by Albert Barley, the company built an automobile which, at least superficially, resembled the British Rolls-Royce.

Saturn (1984 -) was introduced by General Motors as an alternate for Americans who were attracted to Japanese automobiles. Its debut came during the last year of Route 66's existence.

Studebaker Corporation (1902 - 1964) began in 1852 as a wagon builder in South Bend, Indiana. Many of its horse-drawn vehicles were the covered wagons which took settlers West. The company began building automobiles in 1902, although it continued constructing wagons until the early 1920s. By the late 1930s the company was a major American automobile builder. Its post-World War II models were strikingly modern and boosted sales higher. In the 1950s the firm encountered financial difficulties and in 1954 merged with *Packard Motor Cars* into *Studebaker-Packard Corporation*.

Studebaker-Packard Corporation (1954 - 1964) was organized when these two major automobile manufacturers merged in an attempt to continue in business. *Packard* became little more than a version of the *Studebaker*, and when sales declined its production ended in 1958. *Studebaker* sales continued to decline, and construction of cars stopped in 1964.

Stutz Motor Car Company (1911 - 1935) took its name from its founder, Harry Stutz, who left the Indianapolis firm in 1911 to pursue other ventures. Numerous financiers ran the company, which primarily built sports cars, before it went out of business. Its most famous model was the Bearcat, notable for its name.

Terraplane (1932 - 1937) was the *Hudson Motor Car Company* replacement for its *Essex* mid-sized automobile.

Willys-Overland (1908 - 1936) was organized by John Willys and built automobiles in Indianapolis and Toledo. The company in 1936 was renamed *Willys-American*.

Willys-American (1936 - 1963) was the name adopted in 1936 by *Willys-Overland*, which then was specializing in economy-priced automobiles and small panel trucks.. The company in 1940 began building one of America's most famous vehicles, the *Jeep*, because its developer, *American Bantam*, was unable to mass-produce them. By 1956 *Jeeps* were the only vehicles manufactured by the company, which changed its name to *Kaiser-Jeep* in 1963.

The soda fountain, with its five-cent Coca-Colas and ice cream cones, was a fixture in drug stores until the 1970s. These happy attendants in the mid-1920s awaited customers in the Walgreen Drug Store at 200 Wilmont Road in Saint Louis. (Walgreen Collection)

Company. One of the most popular young singers that seemed destined for both radio and screen stardom was Russ Columbo. He died in the early 1930s when handling an "unloaded" gun. Another personality was Bing Crosby, who became star of his own radio show with the *Where the Blue of the Night* song as the theme. He went on to become one the most important entertainers in motion pictures. Others who achieved stardom on radio were ex-vaudeville performers Jack Benny and the team of George Burns and Gracie Allen, all of whom became big names in motion pictures. Broadway musical star Eddie Cantor duplicated his success on the big screen and also with a weekly radio show during the 1930s and 1940s.

Amazingly enough, a relatively few motorists enjoyed radio programs in their autos, at least through most of the 1930s. Radios or heaters seldom came with cars. Motorola pioneered radios for autos and Arvin manufactured heaters for

automobiles, selling many of them through Pep Boys, Western Auto Supply, or other stores selling accessories. While Route 66 went through areas where the winters brought snow, it also crossed the California desert with its searing, hot sun. A few motorists installed a primitive ancestor of the air conditioner for their trips; it was typically a tank with water that hung on a window and sucked in air to cool and comfort the travellers. It was a good idea but it really didn't do the job.

By the early 1940s, most automobiles came equipped with radios (billed at an extra cost). Air conditioners did not arrive until the late 1950s, and proud owners of this luxury advertised their comfort with "air-conditioned" decals on rear windows. Some motorists tried to impress their friends by attaching such decals even though they in fact lacked this "cool" innovation.

Automatic transmissions appeared on a limited basis in the late 1930s with a "fluid" drive offered

There was so much activity in building roads in the early twentieth century that this supplier issued thousands of cards advertising its steam rollers.

CASE Steam Roller building Country Roads
Price, cash, $1980; on time, $2200.
"Warranted to do all or anything that can be done by any 10-ton Steam Roller."
J. I. CASE THRESHING MACHINE CO., Incorporated, Racine, Wis.

Here is a gasoline service station, typical of those in the 1920s and early 1930s. Note the pump with the glass gas container. (Coca-Cola Collection)

as an option on Chrysler products, including Dodges and DeSotos. Packard, all of whose models were regarded as luxury vehicles, offered an "electric" transmission which eliminated manual shifting at approximately the same time. An innovation in the early 1940s placed the gear shift on the steering wheel column. The shift previously was located in the center of the floor between the driver and passengers, a practice still followed in some sports automobiles. In cars produced after World War II, automatic shifts became available on most automobiles, but only as

an "extra."

By the time the last link of Route 66 gave way to the interstate, only a handful of younger people knew how to drive cars with manual or "stick" shifts.

Few people in medium-sized or larger cities, however, used automobiles to commute to work or shopping during the 1920-1950 era. They relied on buses or the electric trolley cars which charged one-way fares of five or ten cents, and entered downtown areas from almost every direction. As a result there were plenty of parking

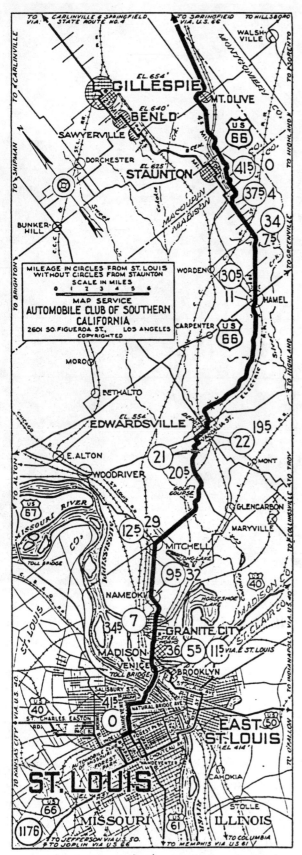

**Copyright Automobile Club of Southern California;
Used by Permission**

places on the streets and little need for commercial parking lots. Coin-operated meters did not arrive until the mid-1930s, coincident with time limits for on-street parking and parking lots. They initially charged one cent for 12 minutes or a nickel for an hour. The trolleys operated on frequent schedules, particularly during the hours of busy traffic. Their disadvantages were the expense of building tracks to reach new parts of a city, and the increasing numbers of automobiles making it more difficult for them to make time on the streets where tracks were laid in the years when there were few autos. As streets became more congested, a police officer was stationed atop a white wooden box approximately a foot high in the center of the street, commanding attention with his whistle and a hand raised, signalling authoritatively for pedestrians and vehicles to move. One very logical innovation came into wide use during the late 1920s and early 1930s: Traffic signals, installed first in the busiest intersections of the larger cities and gradually making their way even to some residential areas of smaller towns. Situated at each of an intersection's four corners, in many areas the first signs had "stop" and "go" arms that mechanically changed, ringing a bell to alert a society not accustomed to this progress. Some cities initially dispensed with the mechanical arms and used green, yellow, or red lights. As the years passed, some signals remained at corners while others hung over the center of an intersection. There were those with "walk" or "wait" directions, and a few had right or left turn arrows. No longer were bells used to alert motorists, who through the years became accustomed to traffic controls.

A predecessor of the electric signal was initial-

Route 66 traffic generally crossed the Mississippi over the Chain of Rocks Bridge, north of downtown Saint Louis.

ly called a "boulevard stop" because it required traffic to halt when approaching a busy intersection. In the case of Route 66, a "boulevard stop" would be erected at each highway or road emptying traffic into the artery. As traffic increased, the "boulevard" appellation was removed and they became simply "stop" signs installed at many intersections where there might be a concern for cars meeting when entering them.

Police officers at the time spent less time in their squad cars and more time patrolling downtown or residential areas, and chatting with citizens as they did so. At Christmastime, people

laid attractively-wrapped gifts around the white boxes on which officers stood at intersections.

The era from the early 1900s until the early 1950s was the time of "downtown" in cities throughout the nation. There were no malls such

37

12th Street, showing Jefferson Hotel, St. Louis, Mo.

A 1920s view of Saint Louis showed 12th Street with the Jefferson Hotel at the right. BELOW: Here is a nighttime view of the Eads Bridge over the Mississippi. Note the trolleys.

26652

Section

B

SEPTEMBER 1, 1993

Desert Star

COMMUNITY

Comics B-4

Classifieds B-5

COMMUNITY BRIEFS

Class of 1953

Needles High School Class of 1953 is
g its 40th reunion and is seeking ad-
or information about the following
tes: Sally Barwick, Jack English, Ron
rginia Fox, Robert Large, Mary Ann
oretta Peterson, Silas Saner, Patsy
Bob Royce and Charlie Gutierrez.
nore information about the reunion or to
information about the missing class-
contact Beverly Howze at (619) 326-
ob Willis, (619) 326-2733, Demarious
t (619) 326-2924 or Eleanor Jo
s at (619) 326-3086.

eyball dinner

Needles High School Lady 'Stangs vol-
eam will host an Italian dinner during
ming week on Tuesday, Oct. 19. The
ill be held on the NHS campus.
nenu includes lasagna, salad, garlic
essert and beverage. Tickets are $5 per
nd can be purchased from any volley-
ver.
nore information or to purchase tickets,
essica Romero at the NHS office at

Needles to host Route 66 event

Over 250 Europeans, drawn by the lure of historic Route 66, will visit Needles on Oct. 11, when
over 130 Club of Ancient Automobiles & Rallies
(CAAR) vehicles follow the old route in CAAR's
1993 Historic Route 66 Rallye.

Members of the group are shipping their classic
American automobiles to the United States to begin
their trek on Sept. 19 in Washington, D.C. The
procession will begin its official Old Route 66 trip
from Chicago, Ill., on Sept. 26.

Activities included along the route afford the European guests an opportunity to see the United
States as never before. Various cities along the
route are pulling out all the stops to make everyone
feel at home.

Chicago has asked the group to participate in the
annual International Steuben Parade. Anadarko,
Okla., is planning a joint powwow with several
Native American tribes and has asked the club to
join in the event.

In Las Vegas, along with a parade down the
center of town, the rallye participants are guests of
the Imperial Palace Car Collection with a planned
wedding of two of the rallye participants in the
middle of a collection of Duesenbergs valued at
over $50 million.

After leaving Las Vegas on Oct. 9, the group
will travel to Kingman, Ariz., to pick up Route 66,
heading for Oatman.

Needles will be visited by the group on Oct. 11.

Sign of the time ... Henri Casanava' displays an "Historic Route 66" highway sign in the window o
Chio's Cafe on Front Street, the original hista in high as home in Ca. 130 CAAR no will

Saluting Route 66, motorists from abroad in 1993 drove from Chicago to L.A. This article
appeared in the newspaper at Needles, a stop along the way. BELOW: This vintage British Austin,
from overseas, visited Williams during the tour. (Photograph by the Author)

as those that came during the late 1940s and early 1950s. Roads from all sections of a city converged on the downtown section, where people found furniture, apparel, toy, jewelry, and other stores — most of them home-owned. Doctors, lawyers, and other professional people maintained their offices in the downtown area buildings, alongside of which were the motion picture theaters, city offices, and central park with a band stand. The railroad station, bustling with people bound to or from cities, both distant and nearby, also adjoined this area. From "downtown" buildings merged into a city's residential area. Retail

This map shows the Saint Louis area as it appeared in 1930. (Copyright Automobile Club of Southern California; used by permission)

stores generally opened at 9 a.m. and closed at 5 or 6 p.m., according to local custom. They remained open until 9 p.m. on Saturdays because that was "pay" day for office and factory workers and the time when the farmers and ranchers came to town. Stores remained closed on Sundays with the exception of a few pharmacies and, after their development, supermarkets. With the advent of World War II many downtown stores started staying open on Friday nights because there was more money in circulation and for the convenience of war workers and servicemen. There was very little turnover among sales people because jobs were difficult to find and they enjoyed their work.

Not until the invention of the mall did "local" department stores venture away from traditional "downtowns," and only with these malls did stores remain open on Sunday, serving customers at night on all of the other six evenings. The "downtowns" accommodated local merchants, a few chain stores such as Sears, Roebuck & Company, Montgomery Ward, J. C. Penney, and a handful of nationwide speciality shops. As a rule these chains selected sites which were "downtown." In those pre-mall, outdoor areas, the owners of property on the side of the street with shade in the afternoon frequently commanded higher rent because of the pedestrian traffic. Shoppers from smaller towns and rural areas ventured for miles to reach larger cities in order to browse at, for example, establishments such as the giant Marshall Field department store in Chicago. An exception to the type of home-owned retailer were the "five and dime" stores such as Woolworth's, operating all over America, and the lesser Kresge's (later Kmart), Newberry's, Kress', and McCrory's outlets, traditionally identified by their red fronts with names in gold letters. While they were fixtures in the "downtowns" of small and large cities, some "five and dime" units were in neighborhood locations.

Department stores in the pre-mall days were decidedly just that; there were departments for toys, apparel, books, appliances, home furnishings, and items, unlike the department stores of the 1980s and beyond which, because of the economic pressures from malls and speciality shops, carry limited merchandise.

A shopper in the early days of Route 66 had a different experience than when that highway ended. In the "five and dimes," or variety stores, each counter was tended by a clerk who almost invariably was a young woman. These stores offered items arranged in compartments separated by glass dividers on counter tops. Few men filled these positions, but worked as assistant managers or stock clerks. The counters, encompassing the clerk and forming a small department, displayed toys, cosmetics, stationery, toothpaste, first-aid items, and even clothing for children. There was always a confectionery counter, where attendants used scoops to fill bags according to order for weight and choices, with candy that sold for 10 cents to 25 cents a pound. The clerks could authoritatively answer questions about the merchandise, ring up the sale, and package the purchase, letting the customer go to another

41

This attendant used a pick to flake ice from a block in the 1930s, when there were few ice cube makers. (Coca-Cola Archives)

specialized counter. The cost of an item ranged from a penny upward, but it was difficult to find an article that cost more than $2. The prices at the time, however, were not necessarily bargains since the grand sum of 50 cents an hour then was considered relatively "big" pay for many jobs. The young women at the variety store counters received pay below the average wages prevalent in other retail sales outlets, but they often managed to support a small family and moved on to higher paying positions when and if they were lucky enough to find one in an era when jobs were scarce and many sought them.

Some variety stores even provided pianos, including women to play them, so that shoppers could hear the melody of new songs before purchasing the sheet music. In many cities, the buildings for "five and dimes" often were fairly large, comprising a basement, main floor, and second or

42

Blue Bonnet Court
4½ Miles West of
St. Louis
Missouri

SLEEP AND REST

IN THE BEST

On U. S. City 66 - One half Mile East of By pass at Junction of U. S. 66 and 61

This motor court near Saint Louis used its location on Route 66 to attract over-nighters. Its layout was similar to many motels in the pre-franchise era of the 1930s and 1940s.

third stories — all jammed with many small items. In the late 1940s, "super" drug stores were born, with large stocks and central checkout stands at their fronts. Their success prompted the variety stores to discontinue individual counter "departments" and also check-out cashiers for self-service customers.

Drug stores also did much more than fill prescriptions during this era. They provided counters for cosmetics, film, candy, and miscellaneous gifts. Sales people at each counter helped the customer by answering questions in detail, making suggestions, packaging the purchase, and ringing up the sale at the cash register.

Soda fountains, the name at the time for lunch counters, operated at the variety and drug stores. For five cents, one could buy a Coca-Cola, made on the spot by a smiling waiter or waitress using syrup and carbonated water. Sandwiches,

prepared on work areas on the inside part of the counter, went for as little as 10 cents. The larger pharmacies and variety stores also offered the luxury of service in a booth, for which on rare occasions a grateful waiter or waitress might receive a tip of 5 or 10 cents if the customer was well-heeled. Pharmacies, like the variety stores, also offered counters selling numerous items. The

LOG CITY CAMP
33 miles east of Joplin -- 44 miles west of Springfield
Located on U. S. 66   Official A. A. A. Camp
MODERN COTTAGES   ♦   EXCELLENT MEALS
Finest Coffee on the Highway
W. M. BAKER, Owner

Meramec Caverns, on the Meramec River at Stanton, was a legendary hiding place for bandit Jesse James. It was opened to the public in 1933. (Both Photographs: Meramec Caverns Collection)

clerk at the cosmetic counter, herself immaculately groomed, would happily help a customer select make-up and even demonstrate the techniques of properly applying it. A customer would not dare to go behind the counter to select an item from a glass counter or a wall cabinet. Self-service pharmacies and variety stores did not exist until the late 1940s. Soda fountains remained in operation at these stores for a few more years, but were removed to make room for merchandise which brought bigger profits. The arrival of fast food outlets, beginning in the 1950s with bargain-priced hamburgers, doomed soda fountains completely except for the few which retained them as novelties.

The typical family in the early 1920s bought their groceries at a small store, often in a neighborhood, where the clerks, usually a husband and

Six wheelers - easy on highways - fast - and sure footed when the going is tough.

Route 66 not only opened new vistas for visitors, but it also helped develop the trucking industry. This is an early 1930s photograph of vehicles used by Consolidated Truck Lines, predecessor of CF Motor Freight. Note that because of narrow and winding roads, the trucks lacked trailers. (CF Motor Freight Archives)

wife who owned the establishment, took an item from shelves that almost reached the ceiling and placed it on the counter as the customer made a choice. In the larger markets or general stores, there were several clerks who gave individual attention to each customer selecting food from a shelf. This continued until the shopper had all of the desired items. Self-service was not part of this operation. An immense step forward in grocery operations came almost coincidentally with the beginning of Route 66. This was the self-service grocery store, which was larger than the mom-and-pop shops and because of the volume and fewer clerks required permitted lower prices. This innovation was pioneered by such chains as Piggly Wiggly, Safeway, Kroger, and A & P (for the Great Atlantic and Pacific Tea Company).

By the way, until the 1960s most candy bars were twice as large as in the 1970s and thereafter and cost just a nickel. If one made the purchase at a supermarket or chain drug store, the goodies were three for 10 cents.

Consider, however, that the average wage-earner received only 30 to 50 cents an hour, at least until the 1940s.

At this time there were no Wal-Marts, Kmarts, Targets, or other retail establishments offering mass-marketing and discount prices. Shoppers expected to pay the price tagged on an item whether they patronized a small-town retailer or one in a large city. The large "discount" stores that sold lower than the list price or even at a loss to attract customers came only in the late 1950s and early 1960s. As a newspaper reporter and writer, this

Comfort and service for the motorist became important for marketing gasoline. Frank Phillips (in dark suit), founder of Phillips Petroleum, and executive K.S. Adams took time out on Route 66 to pose with the registered nurses who cruised highways, assisted travellers, and checked stations for cleanliness. (Phillips Petroleum Company Archives) BELOW: With better highways, Ford began to produce more luxurious automobiles. This a 1933 Lincoln; note the trunk at the rear. (Ford Motor Company Archives)

INFORMATION PAGES

RATES FROM SAN BERNARDINO TO MANY NORTH AMERICAN CITIES

Rates For Points Not Listed Below May be Obtained by Dialing "0"

FOR OUT-OF-TOWN CALLS DIAL "0"

TO:	Station-to-Station DAY (Except Sunday) 4:30 A.M. To 6:00 P.M.	Station-to-Station NIGHT 6:00 P.M. To 4:30 A.M. And Sunday	Person-to-Person DAY (Except Sunday) 4:30 A.M. To 6:00 P.M.	Person-to-Person NIGHT 6:00 P.M. To 4:30 A.M. And Sunday	TO:	Station-to-Station DAY (Except Sunday) 4:30 A.M. To 6:00 P.M.	Station-to-Station NIGHT 6:00 P.M. To 4:30 A.M. And Sunday	Person-to-Person DAY (Except Sunday) 4:30 A.M. To 6:00 P.M.	Person-to-Person NIGHT 6:00 P.M. To 4:30 A.M. And Sunday
Akron, Ohio	$2.35	$1.85	$3.30	$2.80	Idaho Falls, Idaho	$1.50	$1.10	$2.10	$1.70
Albuquerque, N. M.	1.40	1.00	1.95	1.55	Indianapolis, Ind.	2.25	1.80	3.15	2.70
Alhambra, Calif.	.40	.35	.50	.50	Inglewood, Calif.	.45	.35	.55	.50
Amarillo, Texas	1.65	1.25	2.30	1.90	Kansas City, Mo.	2.00	1.60	2.80	2.40
Anaheim, Calif.	.35	.35	.45	.45	Laguna Beach, Calif.	.40	.35	.50	.50
Annapolis, Md.	2.45	1.95	3.40	2.90	Las Vegas, Nev.	.75	.45	1.05	.75
Arcadia, Calif.	.35	.35	.45	.45	Lincoln, Neb.	1.95	1.55	2.75	2.35
Arrowhead, Calif.	.10	.10	.15	.15	Loma Linda, Calif.	.05	.05	Not	Quoted
Atlanta, Ga.	2.30	1.80	3.25	2.75	Long Beach, Calif.	.45	.35	.55	.50
Avalon, Calif.	.60	.35	.75	.60	Los Angeles, Calif.	.45	.35	.55	.50
Bakersfield, Calif.	.85	.45	1.05	.70	Louisville, Ky.	2.25	1.80	3.15	2.70
Baltimore, Md.	2.45	1.95	3.40	2.90	Memphis, Tenn.	2.15	1.70	3.00	2.55
Banning, Calif.	.25	.25	.30	.30	Merced, Calif.	1.20	.75	1.60	1.15
Beverly Hills, Calif.	.45	.35	.55	.50	Miami, Fla.	2.45	1.95	3.40	2.90
Big Bear Lake, Calif.	.25	.25	.30	.30	Milwaukee, Wis.	2.20	1.75	3.10	2.65
Big Pine, Calif.	1.05	.65	1.40	1.00	Minneapolis, Minn.	2.10	1.65	2.95	2.50
Birmingham, Ala.	2.25	1.80	3.15	2.70	Monrovia, Calif.	.35	.35	.45	.45
Bishop, Calif.	1.10	.70	1.45	1.05	Montebello, Calif.	.40	.35	.50	.50
Boise, Idaho	1.45	1.05	2.00	1.60	Newark, N. J.	2.50	2.00	3.50	3.00
Boston, Mass.	2.50	2.00	3.50	3.00	New Orleans, La.	2.20	1.75	3.10	2.65
Brawley, Calif.	.80	.45	1.00	.70	Newport Beach, Calif.	40	.35	.50	.50
Brea, Calif.	.30	.30	.40	.40	New York City, N. Y.	2.50	2.00	3.50	3.00
Bridgeport, Conn.	2.50	2.00	3.50	3.00	Ogden, Utah	1.35	.95	1.85	1.45
Buena Park, Calif.	.35	35	.45	.45	Omaha, Neb.	1.95	1.55	2.75	2.35
Butte, Mont.	1.60	1.20	2.25	1.85	Ontario, Calif.	.20	.20	.25	.25
Canoga Park, Calif.	.55	.35	.65	.55	Orange, Calif.	.30	.30	.40	.40
Cedar City, Utah	1.05	.70	1.40	1.05	Palm Springs, Calif.	.35	.35	.45	.45
Cheyenne, Wyo.	1.60	1.20	2.25	1.85	Pasadena, Calif.	.40	.35	.50	.50
Chicago, Ill.	2.20	1.75	3.10	2.65	Philadelphia, Pa.	2.50	2.00	3.50	3.00
Chula Vista, Calif.	.70	.35	.85	.65	Phoenix, Ariz.	1.00	65	1.35	1.00
Cincinnati, Ohio	2.30	1.80	3.25	2.75	Pittsburgh, Pa.	2.40	1.90	3.35	2.85
Cleveland, Ohio	2.35	1.85	3.30	2.80	Pomona, Calif.	.25	.25	30	.30
Colorado Springs, Colo.	1.55	1.15	2.15	1.75	Portland, Ore.	1.65	1.25	2.30	1.90
Colton, Calif.	.05	.05	Not	Quoted	Redlands, Calif.	.10	.10	.15	.15
Compton, Calif.	.45	.35	.55	.50	Reno, Nev.	1.10	.75	1.45	1.10
Corona, Calif.	.20	.20	.25	.25	Rialto, Calif.	.05	.05	Not	Quoted
Covina, Calif.	.30	.30	.40	.40	Riverside, Calif.	.10	.10	.15	.15
Crestline, Calif.	.10	.10	.15	.15	Sacramento, Calif.	1.40	1.00	1.85	1.45
Culver City, Calif.	.45	.35	.55	.50	St. Louis, Mo.	2.15	1.70	3.00	2.55
Dallas, Texas	1.90	1.50	2.65	2.25	Salt Lake City, Utah	1.30	.90	1.80	1.40
Dayton, Ohio	2.30	1.80	3.25	2.75	San Diego, Calif.	.65	.35	.80	.60
Denver, Colo.	1.60	1.20	2.25	1.85	San Francisco, Calif.	1.40	1.00	1.85	1.45
Des Moines, Iowa	2.05	1.65	2.85	2.45	San Jose, Calif.	1.30	.85	1.75	1.30
Detroit, Mich.	2.35	1.85	3.30	2.80	San Luis Obispo, Calif.	1.05	.65	1.40	1.00
Dubuque, Iowa	2.15	1.70	3.00	2.55	Santa Ana, Calif.	.35	.35	.45	.45
Duluth, Minn.	2.15	1.70	3.00	2.55	Santa Barbara, Calif.	.85	.45	1.05	.70
El Centro, Calif.	.85	.45	1.05	.70	Santa Monica, Calif.	.50	.35	.60	.55
El Monte, Calif.	.35	.35	.45	.45	Savannah, Ga.	2.40	1.90	3.35	2.85
El Paso, Texas	1.45	1.05	2.00	1.60	Seattle, Wash.	1.70	1.30	2.40	2.00
Elsinore, Calif.	.25	.25	.30	.30	Spokane, Wash.	1.70	1.30	2.40	2.00
Etiwanda, Calif.	.15	.15	.20	.20	Springfield, Ill.	2.15	1.70	3.00	2.55
Fallbrook, Calif.	.45	.35	.55	.50	Stockton, Calif.	1.35	.90	1.80	1.35
Fontana, Calif.	.10	.10	.15	.15	Toledo, Ohio	2.30	1.80	3.25	2.75
Fort Worth, Texas	1.90	1.50	2.65	2.25	Tucson, Ariz.	1.10	.75	1.45	1.10
Fresno, Calif.	1.05	.65	1.40	1.00	Tulsa, Okla.	1.95	1.55	2.75	2.35
Fullerton, Calif.	.30	.30	.40	.40	Upland, Calif.	.20	.20	.25	.25
Glendale, Calif.	.45	.35	.55	.50	Ventura, Calif.	.75	.40	.90	.65
Highland, Calif.	.05	.05	Not	Quoted	Washington, D. C.	2.45	1.95	3.40	2.90
Huntington Beach, Calif.	.45	.35	.55	.50	Whittier, Calif.	.40	.35	.50	.50
					Yuma, Ariz.	.75	.45	1.05	.75

The Federal Tax is not included in the above rates.
Station-to-Station rates of 25 cents or less are for an initial period of 5 minutes.
Station-to-Station rates in excess of 25 cents are for an initial period of 3 minutes.
Person-to-Person rates are for an initial period of 3 minutes.

Number Please?

When Route 66 began the telephone was celebrating its 50th anniversary, but technology was far from that of the late 20th century. Dial phones were rare and to place a phone call, the subscriber lifted the receiver and an operator asked the question "Number please?"

WITHIN THE REACH OF MILLIONS

This two-piece telephone in this 1930s advertisement lacked a dial: it was typical for the era. LEFT: This page from a 1930s telephone directory showed long-distance rates from the west end of Route 66 to the east.

Long distance were another matter. The operator went through exchanges in major cities to reach the place desired while the caller waited on the line.

Long distance calls were expensive, and a three-minute call across the nation could take a substantial amount of a customer's daily pay during the 1930s. That is why many people used the Western Union Telegraph Service; it delivered a 20-word message for much less money.

Phone numbers in many cities also came with a letter prefix. Thus the number might be GLadstone 8702 or LIncoln 0908. The theory was that it was easier to remember the numbers with a letter.

Party lines provided services in many cities through the early 1950s. The advantage to the customer was that the monthly charge was lower because of sharing, but there were the problems of party-liners not being able to call with a line in use. The most widely-used telephone was the two-piece one that provided for the caller to hold a heavy receiver in one hand and speak into a separate instrument. One-piece phones came into use in the mid-1930s, but they required an additional fee until the 1950s. Then they came into universal use and the two-piece phones became antiques.

Touch-tone phones came in the late 1960s and 1970s. Until the 1970s it was illegal to use any telephone instrument unless it was the phone company's. If one wanted a colored or other non-standard phone, there was an initial charge plus a monthly fee. The change in the law gave birth to a new industry, selling telephones of all sizes, colors, and configurations.

In the 1960s the lettered prefixes were vanishing, despite protests by telephone subscribers who liked them. Coincidentally, there were area codes permitting subscribers to dial directly any where in the world. With this electronic dialing, rates for calling long distances dropped spectacularly.

Telephone answering machines made their debut in the early 1960s.

Alexander Graham Bell would enjoy modern telephones and what they can do.

author interviewed many interesting people, including Ariel and Will Durant, Howard Hughes, Bob Hope, Earl Warren, Dr. Charles Richter, and Humphrey Bogart — not to mention an assortment of Olympic Gold Medal winners and United States senators and Congressional representatives.

Despite this, my most important story as a journalist, from the standpoint of consequences, was the 1952 cutting of the ribbon that opened the Lakewood (California) Center Mall. I speculated at the time how such a place could operate when it was five miles from Long Beach's downtown shopping district, which for nearly half a century had attracted customers for miles around.

A year later, shoppers had all but abandoned downtown Long Beach and the story was repeated in cities across the nation when merchants in older sections vainly tried to compete with those in the malls. Buses and trolleys were on their way out because it was difficult for them to serve the sprawling housing tracts which were developed after World War II. The first post-war homes often came with single-car garages, but soon builders provided space for two cars or more to accommodate a society that, more than ever, was taking to the wheels. Malls provided extensive parking, and the parking was free.

The daily afternoon newspaper during the

This photograph of a Humble Oil Company station, probably made in the 1940s, shows how relatively small units were nestled on corners during the Route 66 era. Until the late 1940s, self-service stations were non-existent. (Exxon Company Archives)

"downtown" era was a major part of American life, and it was faithfully delivered at approximately 4 p.m. by a bicycle-riding carrier so that the household could read it before supper. Morning newspapers were in the minority and circulated mainly to executives or professionals who because of their schedules had more time at breakfast.

Larger cities had boys and even men and women selling individual copies of newspapers on all four corners of downtown streets; for some reason, few girls neither wanted or could "get" a corner. In busy cities a single corner would have multiple vendors with competing newspapers. In many cities, newspapers issued several editions during each day to provide the latest events in those pre-radio news days. They shouted five or six word condensations of the major news stories to attract buyers who did not want to wait for delivery of the afternoon paper. When major news events occurred, newspapers issued "extras" and the vendors were able to shout the "read all about it" headlines in the manner that are so memorable in vintage motion pictures. Some vendors remained at their jobs for years, making friends with regular customers and earning a living. Street newspaper dealers survive, of course, in centers such as New York City and London.

From the teens through the early 1970s, even smaller cities had two or more newspapers, some of them competing for afternoon customers.

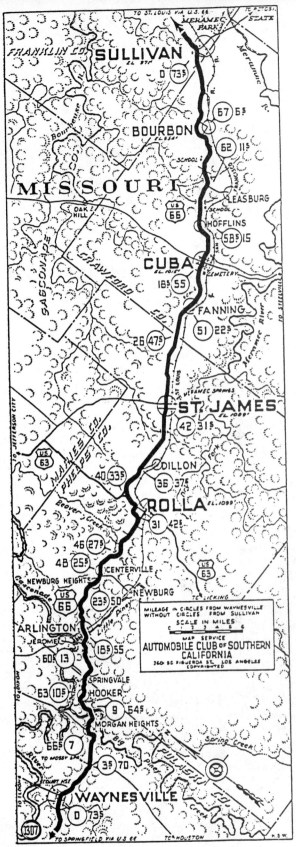

Copyright Automobile Club of Southern California;
Used by Permission

Situated on Route 66 eight miles west of Rolla, this motel survived the arrival of the interstate but the restaurant was torn down to make way for the I-44. (Rolla Route 66 Souvenirs) BELOW: This service station was typical of those erected along Route 66 during the 1920s and early 1930s. (Shell Oil Company Archives)

This photograph shows Hooker Cut between Waynesville and Rolla, in the 1930s and still one of the most beautiful spots on Old Route 66. (Rolla Route 66 Souvenirs)

Television, with its increasing emphasis on news starting in the 1960s, doomed most afternoon dailies.

Radio, beginning during the 1920s, gradually became part of America's social structure. Despite relatively high price tags at the time, the public began buying radio sets, which came in luxurious mahogany cabinets and used light bulb-like tubes which eventually needed replacing; transistors arrived during the 1950s, replacing the tubes. Electric phonographs did not come until the late 1930s. Instead, most homes had a Victrola, an instrument housed in a beautiful wooden cabinet. By winding its mechanism and placing a record that rotated at 78 turns per minute, one could enjoy all types of music without going to a concert hall. Records of 45 revolutions per minute and the longer playing 33 rpms came in the 1940s and 1950s.

In 1926, when Route 66 officially came into being, the popular songs included Irving Berlin's *Because I Love You* and *Bye Bye Blackbird* by Mort Dixon. In regard to motion pictures, *Don Juan* starring John Barrymore drew audiences to theaters — still a year away from the "talkies" stage. Baseball was just as popular then as it would be decades later. This was the year that St. Louis beat New York, four games to three, winning the World Series. Heavyweight champion Gene Tunney defeated Jack Dempsey in a 10-

53

This 1959 scene shows Rolla's Pine Street, over which Route 66 travelled. BELOW: This Sinclair Pennant at Rolla was one of the more spectacular places for lodging in the Route 66 era. It was torn down in the 1980s. (Both Photographs: Rolla Route 66 Souvenirs)

HOTEL OF SINCLAIR PENNANT TAVERN SYSTEM
Columbia, Mo. (On U. S. Highways 40 and 63) — Rolla, Mo. (On U. S. Highways 66 and 63)

SINCLAIR PENNANT TAVERNS

Miami, Okla.	U. S. Highway 66	Tulsa, Okla.	U. S. Highway 66
Rolla, Mo.	U. S. Highways 66 and 63	Springfield, Mo.	U. S. Highway 66
Columbia, Mo.	U. S. Highways 40 and 63	Des Peres, Mo. (on Manchester Road near St. Louis)	U.S. Hy. 50

round bout, and in Pasadena's Rose Bowl Alabama beat Washington 20 to 19. Frank Lockhart won the Indianapolis 500, averaging an unbelievable 95.9 miles per hour.

Speaking of automobiles, and in a sense that was what Route 66 was about, they preoccupied many American families because of the freedom they brought. The low-priced Ford Model T, as well as its successor, the Model A, made it possible for almost every family to own a car. That allowed, depending on the place of residence, family outings to lakes, mountains, parks, and nearby cities. There were few coast-to-coast or even midwest-to-coast treks because decent highways were virtually non-existent. The birth of Route 66 ended all of this.

Even though automobiles were more popular than ever, every family did not have a car, thanks to good public transportation. Typical homes had garages with room for one car. Roads outside of cities and between cities were poorly constructed and frequently lacked signs showing directions. This situation caused automobile and truck owners to call on the federal government to develop highway programs that would include systems such as the one which Route 66 eventually became.

Heretofore, railroads were the preferred, if not the only, sensible means of travelling across the continent. Despite the increasing numbers of automobiles that allowed faster speeds and travel over long distances, there was no highway system that provided a uniform quality of pavement or signs to guide travellers.

The proud owners of automobiles wanted better roads, along with posted directions so they

Copyright Automobile Club of Southern California;
Used by Permission

55

could plan trips and know where they were headed. In answer to the needs, in 1921 Congress passed a law designed to develop a unified highway plan. Under this legislation, states could receive U.S. highway funds, if they designated certain routes as federal ones.

Part of what would become Route 66 already was in existence from Chicago to East Saint Louis. Construction began in 1921 and was completed approximately five years later. Almost as soon as the "66" designation was approved it received the appropriate signs. Crews during 1927 erected "66" markers from there to California, even though for most of the way the "highway" existed only in its name; not until ten years later would pavement cover the entire route. For the early years, the only paved portion of Route 66 was in Illinois and the brief stretch that was required to cross Kansas. Each year, however, every state would complete additional miles of pavement, sometimes with concrete and sometimes with gravel or asphalt.

Route 66 originally took off from Joliet,

famous for its state prison which looks like a prison should and whose exterior was used in assorted gangster motion pictures, including the 1980 Dan Akroyd-John Belushi film *The Blues Brothers*. Originally called Juliet, for Shakespeare's famous character, through an error it received the present name because some one along the line thought it honored Louis Joliet, the French explorer. The beginning of the route soon was moved to Chicago's beautiful Grant Park, later the site for the 1933 World's Fair. From there, the highway took travellers to Cicero, home of the notorious gangster Alfonso (Scarface) Capone (1899-1947). The Volstead Act, outlawing alcoholic beverages, became the law in 1920 after years of pressures by some churches, the Anti-Saloon League, and the Women's Christian Temperance Union. The law was probably the most violated one in history as thirsty people turned to bootlegging, the term applied to the unlawful sale of alcohol. Al Capone, a native of Brooklyn, dominated the bootlegging rackets, not only in his home base of Chicago, but also in

The White Castle restaurants were popular on Route 66 from their beginning...

other parts of America. He operated by bribing police officers and city officials. Federal authorities estimated that in 1927 alone Capone took in more than $105 million, not only violating the Prohibition law but also neglecting, of course, to pay income taxes on it. Rival gangs battled each other to dominate the liquor traffic, and in the process caused the murders of at least 250 people, many of them innocent bystanders. An incident which occupied the tabloid newspapers, motion pictures, and television for years afterward occurred on February 14, 1929. Dressed as policemen, five gangsters invaded a garage on Chicago's North Side where seven members of the rival George (Bugs) Moran gang had gathered. Lining the men against a wall, the invaders murdered them with machine guns. Known as the Saint Valentine's Day Massacre, the notorious incident was reportedly engineered by Capone. Police could not legally link the carnage with him, but in 1931 he was convicted of income tax evasion. When he was released in 1939, he was dying of syphilis. Actor Edward G.

Robinson, a gentle man in real life, became a star overnight portraying a Capone-like figure in the 1931 gangster movie classic *Little Caesar*. The federal battle against the Chicago gangsters was immortalized, of course, in the popular television series *The Untouchables* and its motion picture sequel.

From Cicero, Route 66 carried traffic southwesterly through the fields of corn to the towns of Braidwood, Pontiac, Bloomington, Lincoln, and Elkhart. Bloomington produced Adlai Stevenson (1900-1965), one-time governor of Illinois, twice the Democratic nominee for President (1952, 1956), and delegate to the United Nations. The highway did and does pass through a variety of areas ranging from factories to farmland scenes that might be familiar to midwesterners, but which are gorgeous to people from the East or West. Here, during the summer and early fall, the corn grows tall and green. In the winter, snow covers the farmlands, and fields look forlorn without the crops. When spring arrives and the seed is sown, tiny plants begin to appear and the

...and the service was excellent! (Both Photographs: White Castle Archives)

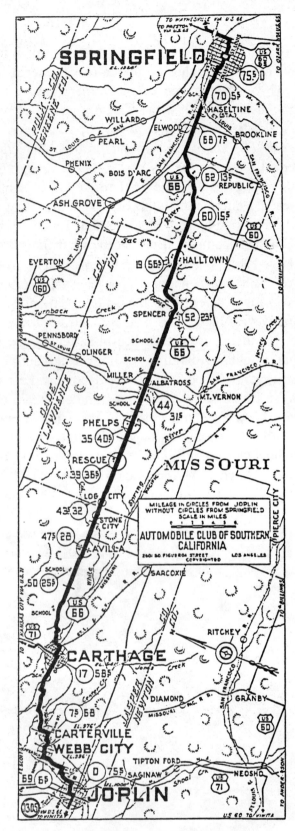

Copyright Automobile Club of Southern California;
Used by Permission

terrain takes on new life and beauty. The first large town was Springfield, the state capital since 1837 and a place rich with the lore of Abraham Lincoln. He resided in the town for 24 years, marrying, practicing law, and buying the only house (still preserved) that he ever owned.

The highway then went on through Litchfield, Mount Olive, Staunton, Hamel, Edwardsville, and East Saint Louis. This area in southern Illinois abounds with industry as well as farms.

When Route 66 came into being, motorists were content with speeds of 40 to 50 miles an hour, the latter being possible with the larger and more powerful cars such as Buicks, Cadillacs, La-Salles, Packards, and Chryslers. At the start, overnight accommodations varied, with travellers initially stopping for lodgings at conventional hotels, which traditionally were near a city's downtown area. These hotels also were close to the railroad passenger depot, still used at the time by many travellers. Wise managers of the hotels soon realized they needed to take care of automobiles as well as the guests. They often made parking arrangements with car dealers or automobile repair shops, who at the time also were largely in a community's downtown district. Parking on the streets also was a possibility, but guests appreciated the security of indoor shelters for their cars even in those days when there was comparatively little crime.

The places that soon sprung up to accommodate travellers arriving in cars initially were termed "auto courts," and many of these vintage hostelries survive today in various forms, a few as motels, some for rent as apartments, and others in ruin. Owners converted some from wagon yards,

built earlier for wayfarers who arrived by horse and buggy.

By the late 1920s and early 1930s, entrepreneurs began erecting increased numbers of motels specifically to appeal to the growing numbers of motorists. "Motel" was a more modern word for motor courts. The identity of just who coined that word has never been established. Several sources claim that it was first used at the Bakersfield Inn at Bakersfield, California (a city which is not on Route 66 but was a destination of the Oklahoma migrants of the 1930s), while others place it at various communities on California's Highway 101, heavily travelled then as it is today.

Early motels typically had one story with as few as 12 units. While the revenue at $1.00 or $2.00 a night was not large, remember that operating a small motel was hardly a full-time job and the owners often lived on the premises. Even at an occupancy rate of 75 percent of capacity at the minimum rate, a motel owner could gross $3,200 annually, which was more than the average worker received. The larger motels, also mostly single-storied, were built in a U-shape with the opening toward the highway and a manager's unit or office in the center. In between the motel units was a space, often with a door, for

Youngsters loved the fountain lunch sections of pharmacies during the Route 66 days. Note the sign offering $1.50 pocket watches for 98 cents. The 1938 scene was at a Walgreen Pharmacy near Chicago. (Walgreen Collection) BELOW: Here is a mid-1930s view of the Eagle-Picher zinc concentrating plant near Joplin, which provided jobs in this area of Route 66.

Central Mill, Eagle-Picher Mining and Smelting Company, near Joplin, Mo.

the guest's automobile. This space had a double purpose, providing insulation from the sounds of adjoining units as well as shelter for cars. Starting in the 1940s, most motels began converting these spaces into additional units, doing the work so skillfully that the casual traveller could not detect the conversions.

At first the motor courts offered only community bathrooms, but soon they provided private facilities. Before such conversions were completed, operators often charged $1.00 without a private bathroom and $1.50 with one. Fifty cents was a substantial sum to mid-America at the time, and it took some consideration to pay 50 cents for the extra comfort. As the 1930s moved on, all motels provided only rooms with private bathrooms. A few units offered a second bedroom for larger parties, and it was not uncommon to have a kitchen so that travellers could save the few dimes that it cost to eat at a restaurant. Rarely did one find a motel that offered a private telephone; if there was a call for a guest, the manager walked to the unit and summoned the traveller to the office. For outgoing calls, there was a pay telephone booth by the office. There were no telephone calling cards until the 1970s,

so the sojourner needed a pocketful of coins.

In 1927, states began improving the highways in order to make them eligible for federal funds. Gasoline tax receipts also increased to fund highway construction costs. Automobiles commenced edging-out trains as a means of vacationing, although it was hard to realize the changes until travellers saw the "Next Time Take the Train" billboards that the railroads erected along highways to stop the trend. Four or more people could travel in a motorcar for a fraction of what would cost if they bought tickets on a train. Although railroad coaches were cooled, motorists rationalized that the savings, combined with the availability of an automobile at the destination and the savings, were worth the adventure of sweltering in the heat. We also must realize that in the 1920s and 1930s few residences were cooled, so travellers hardly felt they were roughing it even though the desert is warm, particularly during the summer months.

Several forces changed social and living patterns in the 1920s. Route 66 was one. Another was motion pictures, which up until then lacked sound except for an organ accompanist who played music that was appropriate for the plot.

Radio Days

Radio was another innovation in America that came almost concurrently with the development of Route 66.

Westinghouse Electric inaugurated America's first commercial radio station, KDKA, in 1920 at its plant in Pittsburgh.

KDKA broadcast the 1920 Presidential election returns from 8 p.m. to midnight. Although less than a thousand radios tuned in, the broadcasting industry was born. Westinghouse promptly established three more stations, including WJY at its plant in Chicago, the city from whence Route 66 would begin in 1926. General Electric's Radio Corporation of America (RCA) and other companies quickly inaugurated radio stations. By the time Route 66 started in 1926 there were more than 600 stations.

As more stations went onto the air, networks began to develop. RCA's National Broadcasting Company (NBC) formed two systems: the Blue Network and the Red (no relation to politics) Network. In 1927, the Columbia Broadcasting System (CBS) came into being with William S. Paley as president. The Mutual Broadcasting System was formed in 1934. In 1943, the Federal Communications Commission ordered NBC to sell the Red Network, which was acquired by the newly-formed American Broadcasting Company (ABC). In regard to programming, music dominated the air waves during the early days. Drama was introduced by programs such as First Nighter and Lux Radio Theater.

The biggest success of early radio was NBC's 15-minute, Monday-through-Friday Amos 'n' Andy, a good-natured comedy about the adventures of Afro-Americans with the main characters portrayed by two white men, Charles Correll and Freeman Gosden. While the program would be regarded as racist by late twentieth century standards, it was so

Comedian Jack Benny (center) went from vaudeville to radio and onto motion pictures. Among those on the Sunday night radio show were Eddie (Rochester) Anderson (left) and Don Wilson.

popular in the late 1920s and early 1930s than more than half the radios in America tuned to it. By airing the Myrt & Marge comedy, CBS eventually was able to cut the ratings.

Radio soon attracted talent from vaudeville and Broadway. These artists included Fred Allen, Jack Benny, George Burns and Gracie Allen, Eddie Cantor, Al Jolson, Ed Wynn, and Rudy Vallee. Starting in the late 1930s, Hollywood talent also furnished major stars for radio. Among these celebrities were Cecil B. DeMille, Bob Hope, and Red Skelton. A highlight of programs was in 1938 when 24-year-old Orson Welles' Mercury Theater radio production of War of the Worlds was so realistic that it panicked Americans from coast to coast.

Daytime "soap opera" serials for adults and evening programs for kids developed.

Most programs during radio's early years originated from New York City or Chicago, but during the 1930s Chicago became less important and Hollywood originated more shows because of the talent there.

News broadcasts developed gradually. The best-known news national news broadcasts of the early 1930s featured Boake Carter, Edwin C. Hill, H. V. Kaltenborn, and Lowell Thomas, each of whom gave a brief one-man program once an evening. Local news broadcasts featured editors reading selections from their afternoon newspapers.

Frequency Modulation (FM) stations, while developed in 1941, did not become a major factor until after World War II and because of its superb tonal renditions, initially specialized in music.

Surveying the inroads of television in 1952, Robert Sarnoff, the son of David Sarnoff who developed RCA and NBC and who soon would head the network, made the pronouncement: "Radio is dead."

He was very wrong.

Television forced radio to fragment and reinvent itself. Radio stations specialized in various types of music, hosts, and starting in approximately 1964, talk shows.

As Route 66 was ending in 1984, radio was alive and well but sounded considerably different.

Gracie Allen and George Burns were vaudeville performers who became stars on radio. BELOW: Radio Station KDKA went on the air in 1923 as the nation's first radio station. This trio used earphones to listen to a program. (KDKA Collection)

Films were indeed "moving," with the players pantomiming. Supplementing the action were titles, which helped the audience understand the plot but at the same time frustrated kids who were too young to read.

The silent era ended in October 1927, when Broadway star Al Jolson appeared in the film *The Jazz Singer* and spoke the now famous words, "Wait a minute, wait a minute. You ain't heard nothing yet!" The picture came from the Warner Brothers studio, a firm which until then was facing bankruptcy. Almost immediately, theaters throughout the world began converting to sound. Among the earliest theaters offering sound was the Sultana in Williams, on Route 66 in Arizona. Color motion pictures, however, were still a few years ahead.

Another major factor in changing American life during the 1920s was the advent of commercial broadcasting. Heretofore radio largely was confined for ships at sea to communicate and for experimental purposes. The availability of home radio receivers and commercial broadcast stations brought new dimensions of drama, music, news, and comedy into the living room.

Better automobiles, new roads, sound movies,

and radio changed the way that Americans spent their time, and they all seemingly came in the 1920s. In fact, there were more major changes in living and technology from 1920 to 1930 than any other time in American history. For the past century, men's lodges, with auxiliaries for women, were a major part of community life. There was the Masonic Lodge, a brotherhood that offered rituals and a comradeship whereby fellow members helped one another in business and in social activities. Most members were Protestants or members of the Jewish faith. For Catholics, the Knights of Columbus was a parallel organization. Both groups had a measure of uniforms and rituals, and both also emphasized spiritual values, at the same time providing centers for fellowship and companion organizations for women. In addition the Elks, Eagles, Moose, Red Men, Independent Order of Odd Fellows, and other organizations provided their members with such activities. Attendance at these and other functions declined when these social and technological advances lured members.

In 1924, just before Route 66 came into being, Calvin Coolidge was re-elected President and America enjoyed prosperous and relatively peace-

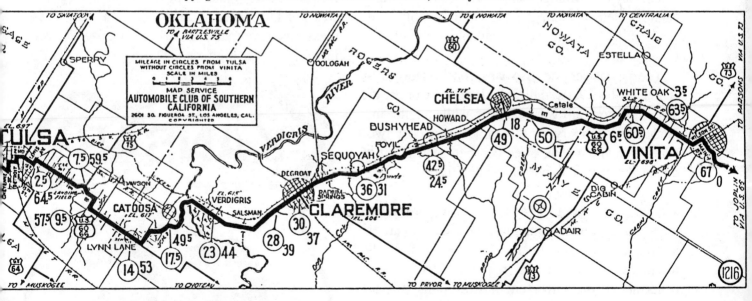

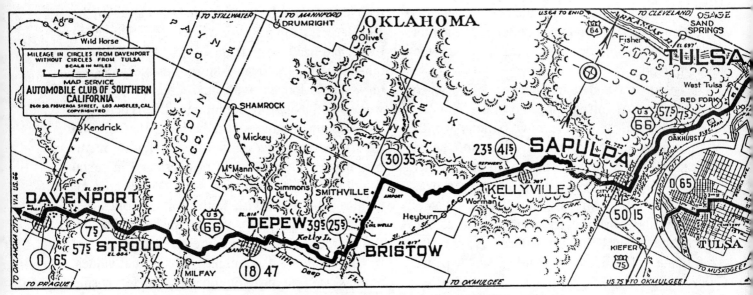

ful times except for the gangsters and racial tensions. Farm prices were good, and thousands of people worked at the booming steel mills, automobile plants, farms, retail stores, and the railroads that served passengers and shippers. Department stores grew larger and more diversified in their products. People who resided in small towns sometimes could not make it over the crude roads to the cities. For them, the Sears, Roebuck or Montgomery Ward mail order catalogs helped them get the clothes, tools, and other things which were available only in the larger cities.

The postal service also was considerably different in the 1920s and early 1940s. The cost of sending a postcard was one cent, while a letter intended for delivery in the same town cost two cents to mail. It took three cents to send a letter out of the city. The postal carriers made a morning and an afternoon delivery on their routes, and service was prompt. As a child, the author mailed a postcard to himself one morning after the carrier arrived, and it was delivered that afternoon. A letter to be sent by airmail required three to five cents above the three-cent tariff. Trains carried

surface mail in Railway Post Office Cars which sometimes cancelled the mail with a "RPO" stamp. Postal clerks sped things along by sorting the mail while the train travelled. It required four to five days for a letter to cross the nation by surface and about two days by airmail, which was used only rarely.

In regard to mail, zoning with a number after the name of the city came early in the 1940s, but the ZIP code system with numbers after a state was not introduced until the early 1960s. These measures were made to expedite mail which was increasing at a high rate. During the 1930s and

This view shows the Reding's Mill Bridge at Joplin. Built shortly after the Civil War, the mill area became a place for swimming, dancing, and dining. RIGHT: This hotel in Joplin's downtown area was typical of hostelries where travellers stopped on Route 66 before the proliferation of motels.

1940s, direct marketers rarely used mail, but relied on magazines and newspapers, expecting customers to clip coupons for an order. Because of the Depression, jobs with the postal service were highly prized and awarded on the basis of tests; there were virtually no layoffs and the salaries were great, considering the Depression. After graduating from high school, the author planned to take the test in order to get such a job. Since there were no vacancies or tests, he went to college and settled on becoming a journalist and college professor.

By the mid-1920s, automobiles were no longer toys for the wealthy, thanks to Henry Ford and his assembly lines which reduced costs. Wealthier people bought the larger and therefore more expensive cars, many of them produced by a new

65

This vintage bridge near Galena was used by Route 66 travellers. (Photograph by the Author)

company, General Motors Corporation.

While more people bought autos, travellers at the time depended on trains for longer journeys. Cross-country airplane flights would not begin until the 1930s. Three major railroads provided service from Chicago to Los Angeles; these were the Southern Pacific, Santa Fe, and Salt Lake (later Union Pacific). Thanks to enticing advertising by tourist groups in southern California, more and more people vacationed in the Golden State and many moved there. California beckoned midwesterners who wanted to escape the winter snows and the Texans seeking to enjoy the cooler summers. Despite more powerful automobiles, the trek was a difficult one because of poor roads. Some motorists had their automobiles loaded on rail cars for the hot, dusty trip over the treacherous Mojave Desert. Roads, which did not deserve the word "highway," from Chicago to the Pacific Coast were mostly unpaved and cars struggled and sank in the mud when it rained. Sometimes the roads took long detours around hills, and going over hills or mountains strained even the most powerful of the autos then available.

These people pressured their local and national leaders to develop highways, not just over what would become Route 66, but in other areas which would make automobile travel easier. Technology was available to create these highways, but make no mistake in believing that the construction equipment of the 1920s and 1930s could build an interstate even if one had envisioned such a project. There were steam shovels to move earth and steam rollers to pack the roadbed, although none compared to the heavy equipment available in the late 1940s. Digging ditches in the 1920s and 1930s was still a manual job, and a rough one for tough men. Machines to do these excavations came decades later.

When Route 66 was conceived, radios and phonographic records, entertained the public with such new songs as Oscar Hammerstein's *Old Man River* and Ira Gershwin's *Strike Up the Band* into the living room.

The year 1927 brought the first Academy Awards to Hollywood. The imaginative *Wings* won the Oscar for the top motion picture, while the awards for best actress and actor went, respectively, to Janet Gayner for her portrayals in *Seventh Heaven, Street Angel*, and *Sunrise* and Emil Jannings for his roles in *The Way of All Flesh* and *The Last Command*. In future ceremonies, awards were made for single performances. Ironically, Jannings won the honor as "talkies" ended his Hollywood career because of his heavy German accent. Returning to Germany, he made motion pictures under the auspices of the Nazis although he was not one. Blacklisted after World War II he died, a lonely man, at the age of 65. In other matters, the New York Yankees shut out the Pirates in four straight in the World Series. Headline news came when Charles Lindbergh, 27, tall, lanky, and modest, in May 1927 made the first non-stop flight across the Atlantic to Paris in 33 1/2 hours in a single-engine plane. President Coolidge dispatched a Navy cruiser to return him to the United States, and on returning an estimated 4 million people crowded New York City's Broadway for a ticker-tape parade.

The Missouri-Kansas-Texas train depot at Galena is now a museum featuring the area's history, including the nostalgia of Route 66. (Photograph by the Author)

Postcards Mirrored Route 66

Soon after 18-year-old Curt Teich arrived in America from Germany in 1895 he took a train trip across the nation with his camera and an idea.

On that trip Curt Teich alighted whenever the train stopped and took photographs of points of interest in the town. Then he persuaded a local retailer, often a five-and-dime or drug store, to sell postcards based on his pictures. At the start, the price was $1 per thousand, with a minimum of a thousand cards. His first trip brought in orders for $30,000.

Postcards were a great way to communicate, both for advertisers and the people who got them. The cost usually was one-cent for a card, and another penny (until the mid-1940s) to mail them.

Teich's quality made postcards an American product. His workers air-brushed out objectionable items and brushed in clouds. In 1910, he moved into a three-story building in Chicago at 1755 West Irving Park Road, and by 1921 added a five-story annex. He died at the age of 97 in 1975 and his family sold the business. Curt Teich retained copies of all postcards that he printed, and they are preserved in the Curt Teich Postcard Archives of the Lake County Museum in Lake Forest Preserve, Wauconda, Illinois 60084.

Motels, restaurants, and other businesses on Route 66 advertised with Curt Teich cards.

Postcard King Curt Teich posed for this picture when a young man. BELOW: This is the Chicago building complex where he produced millions of postcards. (Both Illustrations: Lake County, Illinois, Museum/Curt Teich Postcard Archives)

The Buffalo Ranch, established in the early 1950s at Afton, is still a great place for children to see the big animals. BELOW: Nearby is this trading post. (Both Photographs by the Author)

When Route 66 was going into service in 1927, the average American worker earned $1,358 annually, or $26.11 weekly. This was just over 65 cents an hour for a 40-hour week. Many jobs, however, required five and one-half or six days. Be aware that these were *average* wages. Some workers in executive or commissioned sales received $50 or more per week and lived in relative ease, but many people somehow managed to raise families while earning less than the average wage of 65 cents an hour. The five-day week was rare, and a five-and-a-half-day week was accepted. There was no minimum wage law, and it was common for some people to barely exist. Food, housing, medical care, and other expenses, however, were much lower than a half century later.

While this pay seems miniscule by modern standards, a wage owner could buy food, clothing, a home, automobile, and in many cases finance college educations for children.

A trusty Ford sold for less than $500. If the motorist was willing to pay more, he or she could spend $1,000 and drive off in a Buick, Cadillac, LaSalle, or Chrysler. Gasoline for cars, which averaged 12 to 16 miles per gallon, was 12 to 15 cents a gallon, including taxes. More auto courts were being built along Route 66 and other federal

highways as Americans hit the road in their automobiles. The tendency was to erect motels on the highway at the edges of town, for these areas were away from the more expensive downtown property. One or more restaurants usually flanked the motel; soon there were additional motels and more restaurants in what became a "tourist row."

Motorists soon preferred auto courts over hotels. For one thing, travellers could park outside the unit and carry their luggage for only a few feet. Hotels invariably had bell "boys," who sometimes were in their forties or fifties, and one was expected to tip them 10 cents or so per bag, both when arriving and when checking out. This was a substantial amount of money at a time when a nickel would buy a cup of coffee, a glass or bottle of Coca-Cola, a local telephone call, a cigar, or a fairly decent lunch by adding three or four nickels. There was no such requirement for a tip at a motor court, with its self-service. The advantages of hotels, on the other hand, were that each room had a telephone, usually with 24-hour operator service. Hotels as a rule offered room service for food and featured more expensive items in the dining room. Motor court guests, on the other hand, could save money by dining at nearby

An early 1930s photograph showed the home of actor-philosopher Will Rogers, 12 miles from Claremore. Distributed by the Will Rogers Hotel in Claremore, the reverse of the postcard offered rooms for $1.50 and up.

THE HOME OF WILL ROGERS, 12 MILES NORTHWEST OF CLAREMORE, OKLAHOMA

This photograph of Tulsa was probably made in the late 1930s. Note the service station in the lower center wedged on a corner between buildings.

cafes, which were usually less expensive, and using the pay phone by the motel office for the rare occasion when there was a need to make a call. Motel offices basically offered only a counter for paying the tariff and a rack offering postcards for sale. By contrast, hotels had lobbies comfortable sofas and handsome glass showcases filled with cigars, pipe tobacco, cigarettes, chewing gum, and candy bars. Bell boys on a 24-hour basis operated the elevators, which were not completely automated until the 1960s. Motorists were inclined to forego these refinements because their

overnight visits would be brief so that they could hit the highway as early as possible. As for the telephone booths by the motel office, people on vacations didn't feel the urgency to contact home and long-distance charges were much higher, relatively, than after the arrival of touch-tone service.

Hotels, motels, cafes, and other services operated on a cash basis, since credit cards were approximately three decades in the future. One deviant in operations in those times was that the guests at motels paid in advance and departed in the morning without so much as a "good-bye,"

A 1930s photograph captured the activity on Boston Avenue in Tulsa.

while one who registered at a hotel did not pay until leaving.

By the way, service stations were considerably different than the ones of today. A tall and sturdy glass tank with marks to show each gallon dispensed distinguished the gasoline pump of the 1920s and early 1930s. The gasoline was pumped into the tank, and then emptied by a hose into the car. Measuring one-tenth of a gallon was somewhat difficult since the glass lacked marks to show such amounts. This seldom presented a problem, however, because at 12 to 15 cents a gallon, fractions were hardly a big item. An excellent portrayal of the legendary glass pump appeared in the 1931 gangster motion picture *Little Caesar*. In a chase scene, a bullet dramatically shatters a pump and dumps gasoline to the pavement.

By the late 1930s, these installations were replaced in all but a few rural communities by pumps metered to report accurately the last drop of gas and last penny of the purchase.

In the early days of automobiles, gasoline often was dispensed from a pump on the sidewalk of a general store. Dealers along Route 66 and other highways soon realized they were selling much more than fuel. To encourage motorists to stop, stations provided restrooms, discovering that there were few stops whereby the travellers failed to make purchases. Then they learned that *cleaner*

A 1950 photograph of Sapulpa was made facing east at the intersection of Main (Highway 75) and Dewey (Route 66). (Sapulpa Historical Society Archives)

restrooms enticed even more customers, and proceeded to erect signs advertising this feature. In the larger stations, two or more attendants descended on an automobile to wash windshields, check batteries, oil levels, and radiators, and to adjust the air pressure in tires — all without charge. To gasoline and oil, stations added tires, batteries, and radiator coolants, pressuring drivers to buy these services. They also sold food and soft drinks, helping to please customers and adding a few cents to their profits.

A firm whose history and success was closely tied to Route 66 was the Phillips Petroleum Company, founded in 1917 by Frank Phillips at Bartlesville, Oklahoma, with $1 million. By 1926, when Route 66 came into being, the company's

assets had soared to $266 million. Before opening its first service station at Wichita, Kansas, the company sought a catchy trade symbol to distinguish its fuels and oils. Some one in the company suggested the numbers "66." Then came an unusual coincidence that cinched the decision. A company official returning to Bartlesville in a car testing Phillips' fuel suggested that the "car goes like 60 on our new gas." After looking at the speedometer, the driver exclaimed, "Sixty nothing...we're doing 66!" In a meeting to adopt the name, the official told the story. Asked where it took place, he replied that it was near Tulsa on Route 66.

That highway became the backbone of the company's marketing: "Phillips 66," emblazoned

Patrons of Wimpy's Diner in Sapulpa were enjoying their meals when this photograph was made on October 10, 1935. (Sapulpa Historical Society Archives)

on a highway-type of shield, became the trademark.

Motorists found that the tariffs at a decent hotel in the 1920s and early 1930s varied from $1.50 to $2.50 per night, depending on the city and whether the hostel provided the convenience of a private bathroom so that a guest could forego the

trek down the hall. Motel rates in the late 1920s and early 1930s ranged from $1.00 per night for one person and $1.50 for two, with prices higher in larger cities. As more motels were built, they invariably provided private bathroom facilities with every unit. A motorist seeking accommodations at a traditional hotel needed to enter and inquire about prices and vacancies. On the other hand, motels posted a price on their exteriors so that drivers did not need to alight to inquire about rooms. The signs almost invariably carried "and up" with the sign permitting them to gain a dollar or so in extra profits when there was heavy traffic and only a few units were left. They also had a "Vacancy" sign to which "No" could be added when the establishment filled all rooms, thus eliminating the need for drivers to stop. Econonyminded travellers sometimes would arrive late in the evening, and try to bargain the motel keeper into trimming 25 cents or more off the price so that the proprietor could light the "No Vacancy" sign and retire for the night. This practice could produce difficulties during busy seasons, however, because motoring parties who stopped early might exhaust the supply of rooms. If all the motel units were rented in a town, the choices were to motor on to the next town, which could be miles away, or sleep in the automobile and braving the elements and doing without sanitary facilities.

Motorists had few reservations about pulling off the highway in that era. Remarkably enough, there were few roadside molesters or bandits at the time.

There were no franchised motels, not to mention the convenient toll-free "800" numbers which later would help assure reservations.

When "super" franchised and upscale motels came along, these early hostelries were nicknamed "mom and pop" motels since they were small enough for a couple normally to operate with casual help from their children or neighbors who worked part time.

Motel rates changed little until the mid-1940s, when rates of $2.50 to $3 became typical. The Motel 6 chain adopted its name from its fee of the $6.00 for a night's lodging as compared to the $8

A 1930 photograph shows the WE Auto Camp Store in Sapulpa. L.E. Curd Sr. is with his children, Mayo (right) and L.E. Jr. The man in the window is not identified. (Sapulpa Historical Society Archives)

or so charged by medium-priced hostelries in the 1950s and early 1960s.

A point worth noting is that in the 1920s-1960s era there were fewer parts of towns where it was dangerous for visitors to stroll on the streets than in the 1980s and 1990s. When the sidewalks became dangerous, many inner-city hotels found that business declined.

With many variants in the ownership of motels, quality also was different although virtually all rooms provided warm and comfortable beds. The differences were in swimming pools (few offered them in the early days) and construction (some took shortcuts in using thinner walls). The first motels usually had electric signs illuminated by screw-in light bulbs resembling those on Disneyland's vintage main street.

By the late 1930s, most "auto courts" had changed their signs to the more modern "motel" designation and converted to neon lighting. The new ones boasted more niceties and better furniture.

As motels improved, discerning motorists sought the better accommodations, much to the disappointment of owners of the older establishments. One remedy used in an attempt to lure guests was the "improvement" of a decaying building by installing an array of neon lights, which for night-time arrivals made the lodgings look brighter and more hospitable. Wise motorists learned to slow down and take the time needed to inspect a room to determine if the illumination

Wearing his chef's cap, Whitney Martin, owner of Wimpy's Diner, posed outside the establishment in 1935. (Sapulpa Historical Society Archives)

Dixieland Park became a landmark for Sapulpa residents and a stopping place for travellers on Route 66. Note the glass containers for gasoline atop the service station's pumps. (Sapulpa Historical Society Archives)

obscured a shabby and antiquated motel.

The porches and picnic areas around motels in the 1920s and 1930s were friendly places, particularly in the Midwest where being friendly seems to be part of life more than elsewhere in America. Travellers gathered on warm evenings to exchange stories about the highways, with their hills, curves, restaurants, and characters that one met.

While oil companies began to issue credit cards in the early 1930s, other types of credit cards did not arrive until the mid-1950s and automatic teller machines came in the mid-1970s. Travellers therefore needed to arm themselves with cash or travellers' checks to pay for lodging, meals, and incidentals. In the mid-1950s the Diners Club pioneered credit cards, which initially used a literal card instead of plastic. At the outset of these cards, so few places accepted them that the issuer provided small books with the names of acceptors. The BankAmericard, which really was plastic and the predecessor of the Visa and MasterCard services, became a part of life in America in the late 1950s.

The Round Barn on Route 66 in Arcadia has been a curiosity for motorists since the highway opened. It was built in 1898 by W.H. Odor. Here is the way it looked before restoration. (Photograph by Pam Brix from the Arcadia Historical Society)

In 1928, the Democratic Party nominated Alfred Smith as its candidate for the presidency, and the Republicans chose Herbert Hoover. After a campaign marked by vicious "whispering" charges concerning Smith's Catholic religion, and whether a person of that faith should be President, Hoover won by a landslide. America's first moving electric sign, installed on the *New York Times* Building in New York City reported election results as crowds watched from Times Square. Amelia Earhart of Atchison, Kansas, became the first woman to fly across the Atlantic Ocean. Academy Award "Oscars" for the best performances went to Warner Baxter playing the Cisco Kid in the movie *In Old Arizona* and to Mary Pickford for her role in *Coquette*. In other Hollywood activities, the recently-formed Walt Disney Company introduced a new star: Mickey Mouse.

People in New York spoke about travelling

Restored in 1992 under the direction of Luke Robison, the Round Barn remains an attraction for modern travellers on Old Route 66. The much-photographed landmark is open to the public. (Photograph by the Author)

"west," but to most of them this meant a trip to Chicago.

In most American cities, neighborhood theaters were perfecting what became a tradition until the early 1960s: the "kids" matinee. The programs typically offered two feature films, usually filled with action; a newsreel of current events, one or two cartoons, a short comedy, and a serial with 12 or 15 episodes, each ending with a cliff hanger designed to bring young patrons back next week to watch the rescue and next cliff hanger.

Newsreels were composed of brief highlights of prize-fights, disasters, excerpts from political speeches, and parades. The "news" was very brief and a week or more old by the time it reached the screen. Television and its "instant" history doomed newsreels in the early 1950s.

In addition to an afternoon packed with entertainment, kids often received a complimentary candy bar with the 10-cent admission.

"Service with a Smile"

LEFT: This stretch of Old Route 66 turns into the interstate between Tulsa and Oklahoma City. (Photograph by the Author) ABOVE: "Service with a Smile" was the slogan for gasoline stations in the 1930s. One attendant pours gas and another checks tires in this 1932 scene at a Phillips 66 outlet. (Phillips Petroleum Company Archives)

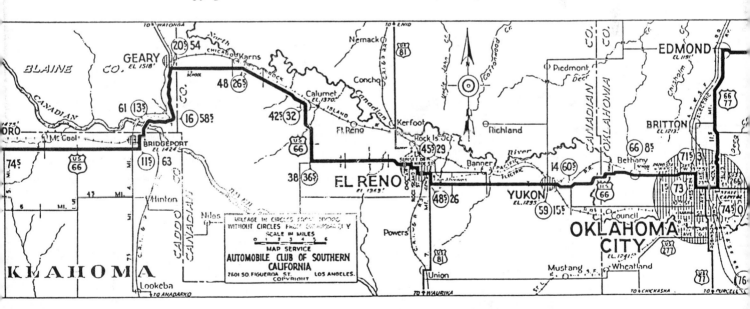

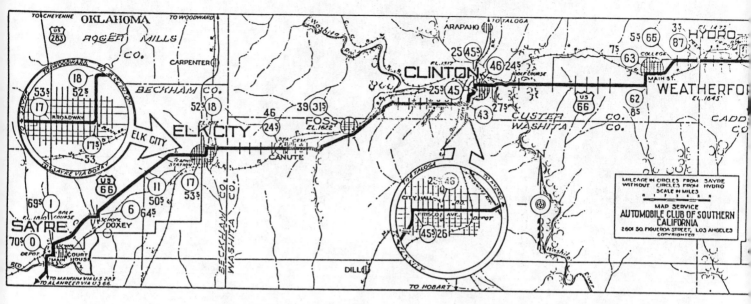

Few adults would brave the interior of the theater with its screaming and clapping, and would wait outside for kids too young to make it home alone.

In addition to afternoon newspaper routes, selling weekly magazines door-to-door was a way for youngsters to earn some extra money. The popular mass-appeal magazines of the era were *The Saturday Evening Post*, *Colliers*, and *Liberty*, each of which sold for the magnificent sum of 5 cents. The young salespeople went door-to-door, sometimes just minutes after a competitor had canvassed the same neighborhood. Besides a commission, kids received points exchangeable for gifts such as bicycles and pocket knives.

Life, the large format picture magazine, did not arrive until 1936 and it was sold at newsstands and by subscriptions. The popularity of *Life* and its look-alike competitor, *Look* magazine, helped doom the established mass-appeal publications.

The exact path of Route 66 varied through the years, unlike interstates which are massive cement and steel monuments. Over the years Route 66 bypassed some cities and touched new ones. In the initial configuration, for instance, Route 66 took what was in effect a detour to Santa Fe after leaving Santa Rosa and then went down to Albuquerque. A few years later, it took a direct route from Moriarty to Albuquerque, saving many miles but missing an encounter with a beautiful city.

Over the years there have been numerous bridges to take motorists over the Mississippi River. The route initially was over the McKinley Bridge from Venice, Illinois. By 1934 travellers were routed over the Municipal Free Bridge (later renamed the MacArthur Bridge) from East Saint Louis. As the volume of traffic increased in the late 1930s, Route 66 changed to carry cars over the two-lane Chain of Rocks Bridge from

TEXAS

US

66

This motor court in Texola, just over the state line from Oklahoma, boasted it was the first motel in Texas. (Photograph by the Author)

Mitchell, Illinois, to the northern section of Saint Louis so that motorists could avoid congestion. Here was the Chain of Rocks Amusement Park, a popular place for family outings until it closed in the late 1970s. Whatever bridge one takes, crossing over the Mississippi makes one feel that he or she has reached a milestone on a trip, whether the automobile is westward or eastward bound.

By the early 1980s not only the amusement park but also the Chain and MacArthur bridges were closed.

Saint Louis is rich in attractions. One can travel by tram in the Gateway Arch, which was built during the Route 66 years of 1962 to 1965 and soars 630 feet above the river near the downtown area. The panoramic view is spectacular. A museum at the base of the arch offers exhibits dramatically depicting the opening of the West.

The river at Saint Louis always has been a fascinating place for visitors with its historic buildings and paddle-wheel steam boats. Steamboats

still take travellers on trips up the Mississippi and its tributaries and down the river to New Orleans.

One of the McDonald hamburger chain's most unusual restaurants is situated here: It is a paddlewheeler floating alongside the docks. One might expect that there would be an admission to visit, but you simply climb aboard and enjoy a meal.

From Saint Louis, Route 66 headed in a southwesterly direction. Just down the highway is Stanton, with the Meramec Caverns, originally named Salpeter Cave by the Frenchman who discovered it in 1720, and an attraction approximately three

Old Route 66 fostered a variety of businesses. ABOVE: The winding highway, often with just two lanes, caused many accidents and the wrecks often ended in junk yards, found in even the smallest towns. This one is in the northern area of Grants. BELOW: Fireworks, with some stands open throughout the year, were attractions for families with youngsters starting in the earliest years. Many are still there. This scene was in Oklahoma.

miles from "66" since it was purchased in 1933 by Lester B. Dill. He found new passages and advertised it from one end of the highway to the other by painting "Meramec Caverns" on barns near the pavement. The cave's advertisements claimed that it was a hide-a-way in the 1880s for the infamous bandit, Jesse James, who presumably was killed in 1882. In 1948, however, a 100-year-old man from Lawton, Oklahoma, appeared and announced he was Jesse James, and had escaped his assassin. He met with survivors of the James gang, who swore his claim was valid. Part of the attraction is the Jesse James Wax Museum in Stanton. While Dill passed away in 1980, the descendants of his daughter, Francena, and son-in-law, Rudy Turilli, still operate the facility.

The highway continued on through Rolla, Lebanon, and Joplin — all comfortable towns with story-book tranquility. The legendary Bible Belt stretches for miles from Chicago down through Saint Louis, through Oklahoma, Texas, and areas in northern New Mexico. It is an area where people are predominantly "born again" adherents of the Baptist, Nazarene, Church of Christ, Assembly of God, and allied persuasions of religions who practice their fundamentalist beliefs with Sundays filled with family worship plus Bible school for all ages and mid-week services. The people then and now are warm and friendly, something of a pleasant surprise to jaded Easterners and West Coast residents. Examining the pages of a phone directory in the 1930s, one

Kingkade Hotel, Oklahoma City, Okla.

This was a mid-1920s scene in Oklahoma City. Note the tracks for trolleys, at the time widely used for commuting in many communities.

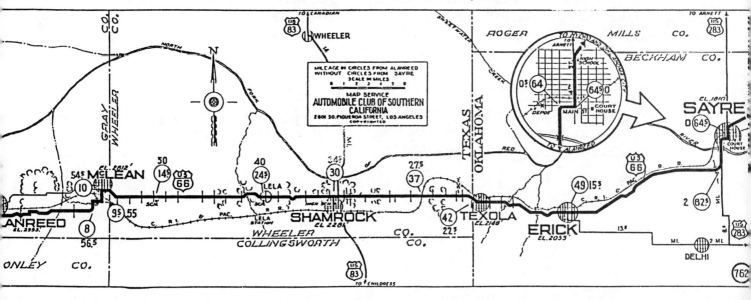

Proud of its Route 66 heritage, McLean tells of its attractions to visitors. RIGHT: A motel and restaurant in McLean trace their beginnings back to Route 66 days. (Both Photographs by the Author)

finds numerous churches of the fundamentalist faiths and a scattering of Methodist, Presbyterian, Episcopal, or similar "liberal" places of worship. There were few Catholic or Jewish congregations. When visiting in the Bible Belt, the author once asked a family friend how these churches came to be. An expected answer would have been that some individuals came through delivering particularly wonderful sermons or revivals that seeded the churches, or that individuals graciously donated the church buildings. "Because we are (the only ones) right!" came the answer. And that was the end of our conversation regarding religion.

In southern Missouri, one finds overtones of the Civil War in the statues and museums. The Confederates and Union forces turned sections of

the state into battlegrounds during that tragic war, and there are cemeteries and historical monuments as reminders. The author's great grandparents, Thomas and Drusilla Payne, resided in Joplin briefly after the war and our family knew that he superintended a local mine. Over a course of many trips through the area, the author determined it would have been a lead or clay mine since there once were many of both in the area. There are many abandoned tunnels that catacomb Joplin. In discussing this book with a colleague, Delwin Jones, an interesting point came up. His great-grandfather also worked in the Joplin mines just after the Civil War, and we speculated that the town then was so small that their paths would indubitably have crossed.

From the interstate, one can see Joplin's

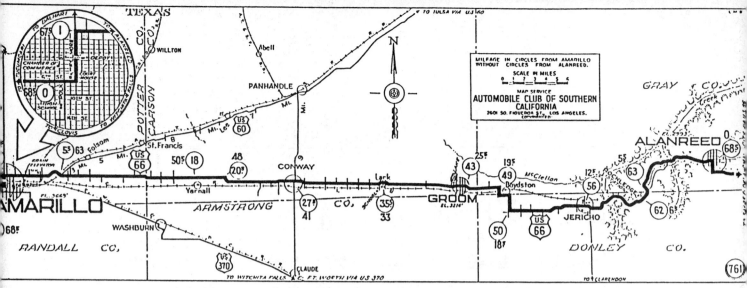

modern motels. By strolling along Old Route 66, however, one sees early motels that remind visitors of the 1930s and 1940s. Joplin's older or original downtown area has many picturesque early-day buildings that remain in good condition.

Life in the smaller towns on Route 66 remained serene and basically unchanged except for the construction of buildings with four and even six stories. The larger buildings were mostly hotels, erected to accommodate business visitors who traditionally arrived by train. As the towns grew, dry goods shops became department stores. These outlets were not of the regional "chain" variety with suburban branches. They were one-of-a-kind and almost always owned by a local family.

Two-car families became common only after World War II. Townspeople rode trolleys to shop "downtown," while farmers and ranchers came to the city on Saturday to shop and took their children to the kids' matinees at the motion picture theater. Not until the late 1940s, with the invention of the shopping mall, were department store branches established.

Americans felt relatively secure in the

This Phillips 66 service station, typical of those dating back to the beginning of Route 66, is preserved in McLean. (Photograph by the Author)

UNITED STATES HIGHWAY NO. 66

SCALE

100   50 25 0   50   100   200   300 STAT. MILES

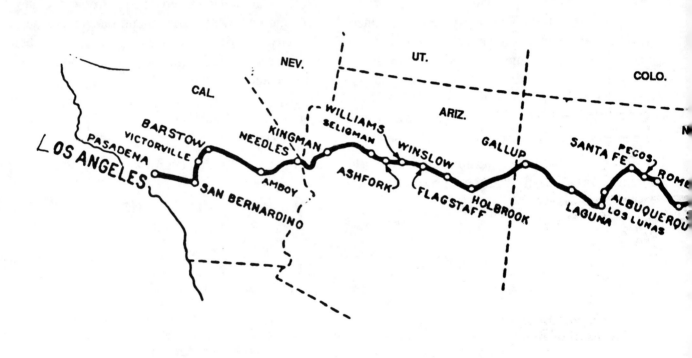

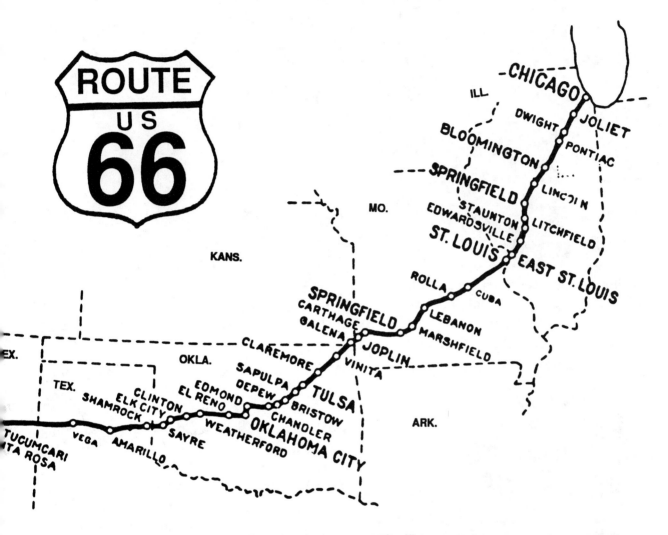

This was an official map of Highway 66 in 1930, before it was known as Route 66 as a result of Bobby Troup's famous song. (National Archives)

The Cadillac Ranch is an art creation composed of tail-fin era automobiles on property west of Amarillo owned by Stanley Marsh 3. One reaches it by way of a service road which was once part of Route 66. BELOW: Tucumcari advertises its tourist facilities with roadside signs all along the highway. (Both Photographs by the Author)

prosperity that followed the end of World War I in 1918 even though one study showed that 60 percent of the population at that time lived below the poverty line. Banks were generous in making loans to buy homes or make down payments on homes, and to farmers and ranchers who offered their land as security. The stock market soared, with prices being bid artificially high by speculators, many of whom used down payments for their purchases with borrowed funds. Banks, which operated with few regulations, also invested deposits, which they were supposed to guard, in questionable schemes. As long as prices increased, buyers could cash in and then acquire more stocks. The danger signs also showed that America produced more than it could consume or, because of tariffs in some nations, could export. One anecdote has it that a shoe shiner requested tips for a stock purchase from Joseph Kennedy, father of President John Kennedy and an investment tycoon, as he went into a building. The elder Kennedy said that when untutored investors were

The Big Texan Steak Ranch Motel in Amarillo advertises up and down the highway that a 72-ounce steak is free to the diner who consumes it and other items with the meal in an hour.

entering the market, it was time for wise ones to sell, and he did so. On October 29, 1929, stock prices crashed and there were losses of $50 billion. That day became known as "Black Friday," and America did not begin to recover until 1941, and then only with the catalyst of World War II.

The Depression hit large and small companies. The stock of Phillips Petroleum, for example, was

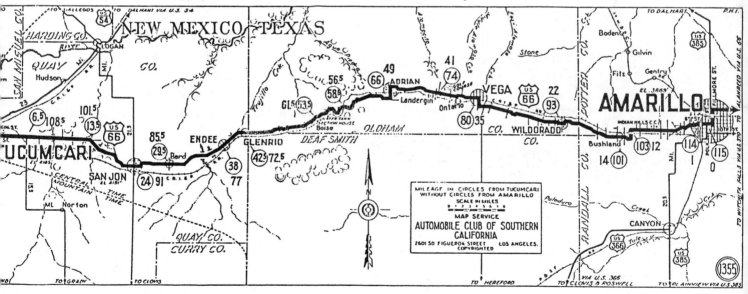

A vacant service station stands by Old Route 66 across from a grain elevator in Conway. (Photograph by the Author)

$32 a share before the Crash; by 1931 it plummeted to just $3 a share. Phillips recovered and maintained its place among the major American oil companies.

A familiar sight on streets was the hungry man or woman who asked what became a question that became anecdotal, "Brother, can you spare a nickel for a cup of coffee?"

And coffee remained just a nickel until the 1960s. Speaking of nickels, it took just five cents to make a local phone call until the early 1950s, when the price went up to a dime, staying there until the 1980s.

This disastrous event caused businesses to postpone expansions, and forced banks to close when borrowers could not repay loans. The prices of agriculture and meat products tumbled, resulting in such tremendous losses in income that farmers and ranchers could not repay loans. The ripple effect produced an economic environment in which the unemployment rate climbed to 16 million people, well over ten percent of the citizens in a nation that then had a population of 130 million — with a proportional work force well under that of the late 20th century when more women held jobs.

Detroit, the nation's headquarters for car and truck production, was particularly hard-hit. Historians estimate that 80 percent of the auto workers were out of work. Henry Ford reduced

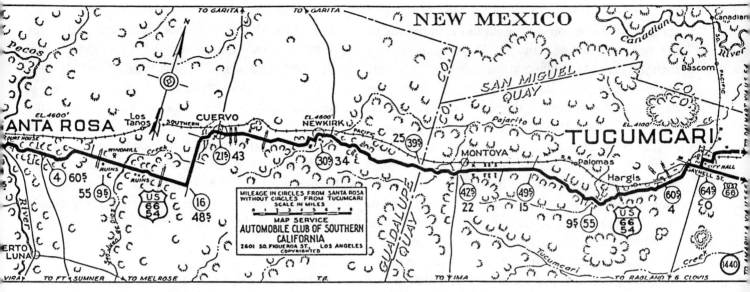

pay to $4 a day from $5, and even then there was not enough work for all of the regular employees.

President Hoover, the man who was unfortunate enough to occupy the Oval Office when the economic disaster came, by his character was unable to cope with the situation. He vainly attempted to revive the economy with loans to business. Unemployment grew, and angry workers marched against the auto plants. In one instance, police officers fired at them, wounding twenty-five and killing four. President Hoover himself was a rags-to-riches success. Born in West Branch, Iowa, he was orphaned as a child. So poor was his family that he went to live with an uncle in a one-bedroom house, and a brother and sister were sent to stay with other relatives. Driving through the area a few years ago, the author came upon the Hoover Memorial Museum where the home mirroring the abject poverty of President Hoover's childhood had miraculously

been preserved. He wondered how the product of such deprivation could respond to the problems of the people displaced by the Depression in any manner except financial assistance. Herbert Hoover, however, had lifted himself from this destitution by earning a degree in engineering at Stanford University and becoming a millionaire.

He responded to the tragedy of the depression by failing to sense the human calamity. The loans made to businesses with the expectation that a trickle-down effect would help the needy failed to boost employment. Hoover believed that just as he overcame abject poverty, so would Americans pull themselves from their dilemma without government assistance as he did and that direct financial aid would humiliate them and make it difficult for them to survive.

In the midst of these problems, Hoover signed a bill that substantially increased tariffs even though economists predicted the legislation would backfire, which it did indeed. Nations raised tariffs on American goods, causing a drop in exports and jobs. In the fall of 1931, more than 800 banks across America closed because of financial instability, in many instances wiping out the life savings of their depositors. There was no in-surance on deposits.

It was in this climate that on May 29, 1932, the Bonus Army, comprised of approximately a thousand veterans of World War I from all parts of the nation, converged in Washington, D. C., to demand cash for their service. The number soon swelled to 17,000 veterans, some with their families, who camped on vacant land near the Capitol. After receiving money to return to their homes, all but 2,000 left. When they refused to depart, General Douglas MacArthur, who would receive fame in World War II, commanded the troops who fired on the men and burnt the shanty town they had erected.

Those people fortunate enough to have kept their jobs found that their pay was cut 60 percent or more from pre-Depression levels. With un-employment so widespread, industries operated at 50 percent of capacity because consumers simply did not have money to buy. Homeless people, meanwhile, erected tent or cardboard settlements, many of which were given the nickname of "Hooverville."

The natives, as the saying goes, were getting restless.

As the 1932 presidential elections approached,

Copyright Automobile Club of Southern California; Used by Permission

Before the interstate, Route 66 led travellers through Tucumcari and helped the city build a strong tourist industry with motels and restaurants. This scene was probably made in the late 1930s or early 1940s.

the Republican Party nominated Herbert Hoover for a second term, and the Democrats chose Franklin D. Roosevelt, a cousin of Theodore Roosevelt, as their candidate. "FDR," as the media and the public called him, won by a landslide, receiving 472 electoral votes with 59 for Hoover. As soon as he took office on March 4, 1933, Roosevelt declared a one week bank holiday and Congress soon passed laws establishing insurance for bank accounts. Prohibition, which enriched underworld gangs that bootlegged liquor, was repealed by the end of the year. The National Recovery Act, with its eagle decals, also was passed in 1933 and established wage and hour standards. The law was found unconstitutional two years later, but employers continued most of its standards.

One of New Mexico's distinctive hotels

MEADOWS HOTEL
LAS VEGAS N. M.
CAFE IN CONNECTION

Henry Ford, expressing optimism, in 1934 restored the $5 a day wage to 47,000 of his 70,000 employees. In 1935, Ford facing increased competition from other car makers, introduced the more powerful Ford V-8, which with variations would be a stable for more than a decade. Then Ford added the larger Mercury and a luxury automobile, the Lincoln.

In 1935, the Works Progress Administration, popularly known as the WPA, also was initiated to give the unemployed jobs in public works. This agency not only benefited those who needed jobs, but it helped put money into the economy and generate more jobs. Moreover, the WPA projects included the building and improvement of many highway projects, including sections of Route 66. Such endeavors probably could not be funded in that way during the late twentieth century because of objections that would come from union workers and profit-making contractors who would argue that federal work would infringe on them. Heretofore, the elderly had little to look forward to when they retired and many of them held onto their jobs because of the desperate economic outlook. In 1935 Congress passed the Social Security Act establishing a national retirement system. Many elderly people retired, knowing they would

The remains of a vintage building on a main street in Tucumcari make a pleasant setting for a recreation area. In the background are the railroad yards. (Photograph by the Author)

Welcome to Hollywood Land

Hollywood blossomed as the world's motion picture capital coincidentally with the birth of Route 66. True, motion picture production, attracted by sunny weather, moved to Hollywood in 1907 and its films and artists were famous when Route 66 opened in 1926.

Technical advances that came almost concurrently with the road helped motion pictures advance from the 1920s onward.

Several factors helped Hollywood to grow into the world's entertainment capitol. One was a wonderful ability of the artists to produce motion pictures that not only mirrored their lives to Americans but also reflected the free American culture to people abroad. Making maximum use of talent and techniques, the artists made movies that proved they had fun with their work.

Almost every little city had its neighborhood theater during the Route 66 days, even though some towns could only support the place to be open

The 1933 RKO film *King Kong* drew crowds to theaters despite the Depression. *Kong* drew worldwide attention to the Empire State Building, virtually vacant since its completion two years earlier, and tenants soon came from around the world.

To Spencer Crump – with best wishes
of Lew Ayres 1986

Photo 1929

ABOVE: Universal Pictures produced the classic 1930 anti-war film *All Quiet on the Western Front*. The star, Lew Ayres (seated) autographed this photograph for author Spencer Crump. LEFT: Oliver Hardy (1892-1957) and Stan Laurel (1890-1965), one of America's most successful comedy teams, appeared in many shorts and feature films.

evenings during the week. Saturday matinees became an American institution during the era, and featured hot dogs and soft drinks along with serials, cartoons, and at least two features — one of which invariably was a cowboy movie. A boy or girl got all of this for one admission price, which was usually a dime until the time Route 66 ended when it crept up to 15 cents to 20 cents. In major cities, theaters took the form of palaces with hundreds of seats and ornate exteriors and lobbies.

One pleasant variation of the conventional theater was the Drive-In, which historian and Route 66 fan Jerry McClanahan says got its start at Camden, New Jersey, in 1933. The number of drive-in theaters spread rapidly. They were wonderful for families, who could buy a variety of goodies from the snack bar and enjoy them in the car, with the sound coming over by way of a speaker hooked to the automobile's window. The audience, enclosed in a car, could talk as much as they wanted without disturbing others. Drive-in theaters were also great for couples who wanted to get to become better acquainted as they enjoyed the movie in a car.

My experience was similar to that of many parents

when I took my children, John and Victoria, to see *20,000 Leagues Under the Sea* at the now defunct Pala Theater in Costa Mesa, California. They fell asleep a few minutes after the picture started.

The attraction of drive-in theaters begin to drop in the 1960s and many were converted to swap-meet sites. A few drive-ins remain, but others are in ruins or have been demolished to make room for other structures.

Mann's Chinese Theatre on Hollywood Boulevard still retains the famous hand and footprints (and even face and other prints) in cement when it was known as Grauman's Chinese Theatre. Here premieres of the greatest motion pictures were and are held.

Modern-day fans also can see the famous Walk of Stars, with the names of celebrities dating back to the silent pictures, on Vine Street and Hollywood Boulevard.

Hollywood films reflected the gangsters, the people oppressed by the Depression, the farmers and ranchers, the police officers the nation at war, how kids went to school, and even how it was to travel on Route 66.

Through the years numerous church groups and other people who believed they knew what was "best" for audiences attempted to provide "rules" for the contents of motion pictures. One organization that sought to govern what audiences viewed was the Legion of Decency, a committee of Catholic bishops in America. Nudity or obscenities were virtually certain ways to have a motion picture condemned. With church-goers pledged to observe ratings, a motion picture with a poor one was a candidate for failure at the box office. Many producers had scripts approved prior to production. The Motion Picture Producers and Distributors of America in 1934 established a code telling what movie-makers could or could not do. These required the use of twin beds for on-screen scenes, even though the couples were married, a limit on the length of on-screen kisses, a ban on showing the methods of crimes, and a restriction on depicting ministers of a religion as villains or comics.

It would difficult, indeed, to mirror modern life accurately with these standards.

Thanks to the courts, these rules were set aside

The Brown Derby Restaurants in Hollywood were meccas for tourists and motion picture personalities from the 1930s through the 1960s. (All-Year Club of Southern California)

and in 1968 a new rating system set standards for children's admissions to motion pictures and finally gave producers the freedom to make pictures as they wanted, and for adults to censor them, if they desired, by not paying admissions.

When people arrive in Hollywood, they see the spectacular "Hollywood" sign on the Hollywood Hills above the community. It is what remains of a "Hollywood Land" erected in the 1930s to advertise a housing tract. The "Land" portion of the sign fell, but "Hollywood" remains and can be seen from streets throughout the area.

The motion picture studios are closed to the public with one major exception, the Universal City Studio Tour (admission fee), which offers a wonderful glimpse of the Hollywood which was and is.

Tours take visitors past the homes of the stars, and stores and street vendors sell maps showing where the celebrities live. Please, folks, let the stars and their homes alone just as you would appreciate your personal privacy!

You can drive by all of the studios — but a reminder: they are factories, and as such are not open to the public.

The late 1940s arrival of television, with its "for free" movies and entertainment, hit Hollywood where it hurts, the pocketbook. To lure audiences back to the theaters, in 1953 Twentieth-Century Fox produced *The Robe* in Cinema-Scope, a process which made the screen much wider and allowed artistic and dramatic effects. The motion picture was a financial success and other studios promptly adopted it or similar processes.

In the 1920s through the mid-1950s, the custom was to sign actors and actresses to long-term contracts, and teach them as they appeared first in

Clark Gable assists Jean Harlow with a bath in the 1932 production *Red Dust*, which help bring about censorship rules of the era.

minor roles and then major ones. When this era ended, players "free-lanced," taking roles at various studios and often becoming so popular that they could command seven figures for a single picture.

While there were great independent motion picture producers during the 1930s and 1940s, these were the so-called "major" or "near" major studios:

Columbia Pictures, started in 1924, and once located at 1438 Gower Street (an independent studio is there now) was among Hollywood's smaller studios until the 1940s when it grew in profits and prestige. Its roster included Glenn Ford, Irene Dunne, Rita Hayworth, and director Frank Capra, who produced the classic films with Clark Gable and James Stewart. With *Tri-Star Pictures*, *Columbia* is now part of *Sony Pictures* and uses the former *Metro-Goldwyn-Mayer Studio*.

Metro-Goldwyn-Mayer (10202 West Washington, Culver City) founded in 1924, boasted it had more stars than there were in the sky. Among its greats were Lionel Barrymore, Marie Dresser, Clark Gable, Greta Garbo, Judy Garland, Jean Harlow, Katherine Hepburn, Buster Keaton, Myrna Loy, William Powell, Mickey Rooney, and Spencer Tracy. It released *The Wizard of Oz* and *Gone with the Wind*.

Monogram Pictures, dating to 1930, specialized in low budget pictures and serials for kids' Saturday matinees. The studio, which really consisted of a spacious ranch for its specialties, cowboy and other action pictures, had a roster of western stars which included Rex Bell, Tom Keene, Tim McCoy, Tex Ritter, and, in his early days, John Wayne.

Paramount Pictures, (5451 Marathon Street, just off Melrose Avenue) dates from 1912 and was the home-base of super-producer Cecil B. DeMille. and stars such as Claudette Colbert, Gary Cooper, Betty Hutton, and George Raft.

RK0 Pictures was formed in the early 1930s and was at the northeast corner of Gower Street and Melrose Avenue. Its most famous productions include *King Kong*, Orson Welles' *Citizen Kane*, and the early Fred Astaire-Ginger Rogers films.

Howard Hughes bought the studio in 1948 and sold it in the late 1950s; the facility adjoined the Paramount Studio and became part of it.

Republic Pictures was established in 1935 and produced mostly low budget pictures, including numerous starring Gene Autry or Roy Rogers — whose films outdrew many major studio features. It went out of business soon after the coming of television.

20th Century-Fox was formed in 1935, and portions of it remain at the southeast corner of Sunset Boulevard and Western Avenue. The studio now is based in Century City. Its major stars during the 1930s were Shirley Temple, Will Rogers, Don Ameche, Alice Fay, Henry Fonda, and Betty Grable, and Marilyn Monroe.

United Artists, was established in 1919 by four motion picture greats, Charlie Chaplin, David Wark Griffith, Douglas Fairbanks, and Mary Pickford. It released features by independent producers in studios they owned or rented. The company later was acquired by MGM.

Drive-In motion picture theaters were places where families and couples could enjoy the movies. This one was by Route 66 in Missouri. (Courtesy Route 66 Magazine)

Universal Studios, founded in 1912 by pioneer Carl Laemmle, this company in the 1930s gained fame with horror pictures such as *Frankenstein*, *Dracula*, and *The Invisible Man*, plus western pictures, and serials for children's matinees. The studio's stars in the 1930s included Lew Ayres, Deanna Durbin, Boris Karloff, and Bela Lugosi. In the 1940s it began specializing in mainstream productions.

Warner Brothers, dating back to 1923, introduced sound to motion pictures and made classic gangster and biographical productions during the 1930s and 1940s. Its stars included Lauren Bacall, Joan Blondell, Humphrey Bogart, James Cagney, Bette Davis, Al Jolson, Ruby Keeler, Paul Muni, and Dick Powell.

In addition to the studios, there were several outstanding independent motion picture producers who released their films through major studios. They include:

Samuel Goldwyn (1882 - 1974) Among the many stars who began their careers with Samuel Goldwyn were Ronald Colman, Gary Cooper, Teresa Wright, Danny Kaye, Will Rogers, Lucille Ball, and Susan Hayward. His productions ranged from musicals to dramas and included such films as *Kid Millions*, *Dead End*, *Guys and Dolls*, and *The Best Years of Our Life*. The Samuel Goldwyn Studios was situated at 1041 North Formosa Avenue.

Hal Roach (1892 - 1993) began his career as a bit player and later produced the Our Gang and Laurel and Hardy comedies. His quality feature pictures included *Of Mice and Men* and *One Million B.C.* His studio was in Culver City at 8822 West Washington Boulevard.

David O. Selznick (1902 - 1965) Before becoming and independent producer in 1936, Selznick was an executive at Metro-Goldwyn-Mayer, RKO (where he supervised *King Kong*), and Paramount. As an independent, his productions included *Made for Each Other*, *Rebecca*, and *Gone with the Wind*, for which he personally wrote much of the script and directed many scenes. His studio was at 9336 West Washington Boulevard, just a short distance from Metro-Goldwyn-Mayer.

Walter Wanger (1894 - 1968), head of production at various times at Paramount, Columbia, and Metro-Goldwyn-Mayer, he became an independent producer in the mid-1930s. His productions included the *Stagecoach*, which made John Wayne a star, and the Alfred Hitchcock thriller *Foreign Correspondent*.

In the 1930s and 1940s, motion pictures were served in a formula, with theaters operating in several tiers. There were downtown houses which showed "first" runs of "A" movies, accompanied by a second "B" picture made with the understanding that it would be the "second" feature. The program was rounded out with a newsreel consisting of a few minutes of an event that was up to a week old, a cartoon, and frequently a short comedy featuring Charlie Chase, Laurel and Hardy, Patsy Kelly, Edgar Kennedy, Zasu Pitts, Thelma Todd, or some other personality with a talent for comedy.

After a one-week engagement, two of the town's top first runs would be combined, along with the shorts, at a smaller downtown theater and then moved to neighborhood ones for three or four days.

Pay scales and production costs were considerably different in the 1930s through 1950s. Most motion pictures cost $500,000 or considerably less; the "million dollar" film was rare and usually spectacular. Top stars ordinarily received $3,000 to $4,000 per week (and were kept busy making several motion pictures each year). With prices of real estate and other investments relatively low, many became very wealthy. In the decades that followed, $10 million was regarded as "low" budget and many films cost millions to produce. In contrast to the stars who received $200,000 or more per year in the 1930s or 1940s, the celebrities of the 1980s and beyond received millions *per* picture plus part of the profits.

Motion pictures have played an important part of our lives. When I was 15 years old I left California with my mother and resided briefly in Lubbock, Texas, a delightful town with friendly people. I was already concerned about people and social issues when one summer day I went downtown to the Lindsay Theater, where *The Wizard of Oz*, a beautiful picture just opened. I noted the Afro-Americans seated in the rear of the theater and thought that this picture was one that everyone should see together, and took a seat among them instead of in the "white" section.

No one, white or black, appeared upset.

Leaving, I went to the bus depot and drank from the "colored" drinking fountain because I thought it was demeaning (although I didn't use that word), to make such differentials, and started walking home.

Along the way an elderly Afro-American stood aside for me, as apparently was the custom. I stepped into the weeds and motioned for him to proceed — which he did after a few words from me.

When I was in Lubbock recently, the Lindsay Theater was closed, the bus station still had two drinking fountains and every one had a choice of which one to use, and I was pleased to visit the city again.

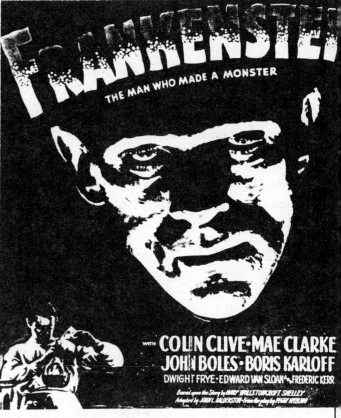

The 1931 film *Frankenstein* not only made Boris Karloff an overnight star after years of minor parts but also helped launch an endless series of horror movies.

Travelers made Hollywood a No. 1 stop in the Route 66 days. Spencer Crump wrote this article in the 1950s for Hollywood newspaper readers.

Citizen-News, Hollywood, Tuesday, November 21, 1950

HOLLYWOOD IS TOP TOURIST PARADISE

By SPENCER CRUMP

A natural glamorland, Hollywood boasts many varied attractions—any single one of which would be considered a valuable asset in other parts of the nation.

Where else in the nation can you—in a single, fast-moving day —bathe in the Pacific, motor through orange groves, ski in snowy mountains, bask in the desert sunshine, and then, as a climax, enjoy dinner in a Hollywood night club?

Snow, desert, ocean, orange groves—all lie within a pleasant one day's round trip from Hollywood. The location department of any studio can point out on a map of Southern California the scenic terrain duplicating the Sahara Desert, the French Riviera, the Swiss Alps, the English coast, and all of the other places where travelers go to enjoy unusual scenery.

Proof of the area's vacation attractions are the 3,000,000 pleasure

These remains of an early church stand on a road south of Old Route 66 in Santa Rosa. BELOW: If being American-owned (left) brings lodgers, a motel owned by an American veteran should go over bigger. The scenes are in Santa Rosa. (Photographs by the Author)

The Club Cafe on Route 66 in Santa Rosa was among the most popular for many years on the highway, but closed, at least temporarily, after the interstate bypassed the town. (Photograph by the Author)

at last receive monthly government payments; this action provided jobs for young people desperately in need of work.

In these years while America struggled with economic recovery, the states and cities worked at paving and widening Route 66.

Speaking of the Depression and workers, during the 1930s labor unions grew stronger and there were strikes in efforts to gain pay raises and job security. The economic fears of the times induced large companies to cut salaries and imposed stiffer working conditions, partly because they feared their industries could not survive the times and partly because they wanted to increase profit margins. When management refused to recognize unions or grant their demands, workers turned to strikes. There were strikes accompanied by violence during which National Guard troops killed several demonstrating workers. Until this time most workers who were organized belonged to the American Federation of Labor, which was vertical in nature with various craft unions representing carpenters, plumbers, electricians, or printers. The Congress of Industrial Organizations was organized in 1938 as an horizontal alliance which sought to represent all workers at a plant regardless of their skills. In 1936, the United Auto Workers, a CIO affiliate, won the right to represent General Motors workers. The Ford Motor Company did not sign a UAW agreement until 1941. Route 66, down in the usually calm Midwest, did not escape labor violence. In 1935, the United Mine Workers under leadership of John L. Lewis, struck the Eagle-Picher smelter near

Galena and violence erupted when scabs intervened.

One industry that benefited from Route 66 was trucking. As the highway improved and made travel easier, the trucking industry grew. While automobile factories struggled for passenger car sales, they sold more trucks. Truck stops, with fuel, maintenance, restaurants, and sleeping accommodations were established. One must remember that this was a time before chain or franchised eating places, and it is easy to realize how eager proprietors were to attract patrons. Chatting and telling jokes, truckers exchanged comments on the best places for meals, and stopped at those receiving the best recommendations. Motorists would select the cafes where they saw trucks parked, knowing that the veterans of the highway in effect endorsed them with repeat visits.

Travelling From Joplin, Route 66 heads southwest and cuts through the corner of Kansas. Here is the town of Galena. While there are stores, some empty in the wake of the interstate, the city still is active and picturesque. The Missouri-Kan-

Once a hub of activity, this complex including a large motel, cafe, and service station on Old Route 66 between Amarillo and Tucumcari stands deserted after the interstate bypassed it. (Photograph by the Author) BELOW: Applying "66" to shops and plazas, businesses create interest. This scene is on Central Avenue in Albuquerque.

sas-Texas Railroad, affectionately nicknamed the Katy, no longer provides passenger service, but the MKT depot is now a museum and is worth a visit.

As it did in its glory days, Route 66 rolls into Oklahoma over business streets and a few residential avenues. Part of the 1803 Louisiana Purchase, this was Indian Territory from 1834 until it became a state in 1907 — just 19 years before the birth of Route 66. Out-of-state visitors today will note that there is an abundance of churches and bumper stickers expressing religious sentiments. Here is the Buffalo Ranch, a favorite stopover during the pre-interstate days and still drawing tourists. Nearby is an Indian trading post, popular long before the designation Native American came into popular usage.

A few miles further west is the city of Claremore, famous for a museum honoring Will Rogers (1879-1935). Oklahoma-born and part Native American, he earned fame as a lasso-twirling cowboy-philosopher in the Ziegfeld Follies. In the 1930s, Will Rogers was Hollywood's No. 1 box office attraction, wrote a syndicated newspaper column which is still reprinted, and presided over

Time for TV

Television was a dream decades before it became a reality for living rooms. Most early experiments involved mechanics, but in 1930 a farm boy named Philo T. Farnsworth (1906 - 1970), who was 14 before he knew the existence of electricity developed an electronic scanning system that could permit television in homes. At approximately the same time electrical engineer Allen B. DuMont founded Dumont Laboratories and made TV sets for the public in 1939.

In 1937 the British Broadcasting System, ahead of its American cousins, began broadcasting over a wide area. The major American networks and the Don Lee Network, owner of radio station KHJ in Los Angeles, conducted television experiments to the handful of television receivers, also experimental. In July 1941 the first commercial TV station, WNBT in New York City, went on the air.

When World War II ended in 1945, television, even though only in black and white, began to spread throughout America. Seven-inch TV screens sold for $400 or more and those with giant screens (12 inches) had price tags of $600 or more. These prices were more than the average workers received per month at the time.

TVs were so rare that families lucky enough to own one invited friends for viewing parties and to let people know their good fortune of having such a wonderful machine. Thet also sent stories of the event to newspapers, which obligingly printed news of the unusual social-technological event.

Coincidentally, TV advertising thrived because the people who could afford sets were in the upper income brackets and had the money to buy the featured products.

Within a couple of years, unfortunately for those who enjoyed the spotlight, mass production resulted in prices low enough for middle-Americans to buy a TV, even though it might stretch their budgets a bit. No longer was viewing television worthy of a newspaper story.

For those whose budgets wouldn't accommodate TV sets, restaurants and bars proudly provided them. They soon paid for them as patrons imbibed for hours as they watched television. Many stores invited passers-by to come in and enjoy a seat as they watched TV. After a few sessions before a tube, customers eagerly purchased their own.

There initially were 13 television channels, all

Sid Caesar and Imogene Coca were the stars of *Your Show of Shows*, one of early television's most popular productions

broadcasting on Very High Frequency (VHF). Approximately one-half of the channels were allocated to a given area and the others to a more distant region. This eliminated the lapping over or interference of signals. Dials governed selection of stations and volume, for this was years before digital controls.

The offerings for audiences would make modern audiences wince. At the outset TV stations begin broadcasting only in the late afternoon when a sufficient number of the people who owned sets were home. News usually was presented by having the camera focused on a news wire machine that was typing out stories. The evening proceeded by showing one or more episodes from serials produced years before for children's Saturday matinees. Stations also relied on older second-tier motion pictures; the movie companies obviously took a dim view of providing even older first class films which might compete with theaters.

Some programs were syndicated comedies or dramas, but in that era before video tape the programs were photographed off the tube to be shown on other stations; this left a great deal of quality to be desired. Among the most popular local presentations were wrestling matches wherein the contestants often wore outlandish costumes and proved to be great ham actors. Some members of the live audience also tried to step into the spotlight. A favorite trick was to phone the stadium and ask for a certain person to be paged, thereby having that person gain a minute of fame over TV. Steve Allen, later noted as an actor, musician, and host, got his start on Los Angeles TV channel 5 with his humorous commentaries on the matches. There were also clowns and puppet shows for kids, plus cartoons, and the Mickey Mouse Club. Youngsters loyally wore their Mouse ears while enjoying the show.

(RIGHT) I Love Lucy with Desi Arnaz and Lucille Ball was the early television series that became a classic and would entertain generations.

The Honeymooners featuring Jackie Gleason and Audrey Meadows, was another comedy series which rated high among viewers.

As the number of TV sets grew, the broadcast hours expanded to 24 hours a day and the variety and quality of programs improved. The sale of television sets grew rapidly during the 1950s and 1960s as audiences were attracted by presentations such as *Your Show of Shows* with Sid Caesar and Imogene Coca, *The Milton Berle Show*, *The Honeymooners* with Jackie Gleason and Audrey Meadows, and *The Ed Sullivan Show*, which introduced The Beatles and Elvis Presley. Comedian Ernie Kovacs brought laughter in using wry humor and techniques native to television.

TV also attracted personalities from radio, whose ratings there tumbled when faced with the big tube. Those who went on to be even more popular stars on TV included Jack Benny, George Burns and Gracie Allen, Bob Hope, and Ed Wynn.

The biggest hit of 1950s TV, however, was *I Love Lucy*, the zany weekly comedy show starring Lucille Ball and Desi Arnaz. Having been in motion pictures since 1935 in films ranging from comedies to dramas, Lucille Ball proved to be the mistress of television with her props, gimmicks, and natural flair for being funny. When *Lucy* appeared, few people would have the courage to interrupt a household with a telephone call or unannounced visit.

Julie London portrayed the nurse and Bobby Troup played the doctor in the TV series *Emergency!*

America loved Lucy!

Despite being produced in the 1950s, *I Love Lucy* has endured over the decades almost as classic books have lasted for centuries.

Two other shows have been shown year after year. One is Rod Serling's *The Twilight Zone*, a half-hour program that ranged from science fiction to comedy, often with a touch of humor and an unexpected ending. Many players who would become major stars or have their own TV began on this program. Among them were Lee Marvin, Elizabeth Montgomery, and Robert Redford; others were top stars of the past decade who wanted to taste TV; they included Brian Aherne, Buster Keaton, and Ida Lupino. The other show was Jack Webb's *Dragnet*, with the producer portraying the indomitable Sergeant Joe Friday who always explained that he wanted "just the facts, ma'm." Modern viewers

might find some of the crimes that concerned Sergeant Friday were insignificant when compared with the modern ones or think that his methods were high-handed in view of recent court decisions. They still, however, are entertaining.

Drama hit new highs with *Robert Montgomery Presents*, *Philco Playhouse*, and *Goodyear Playhouse*. Edward Murrow, famous for his World War II broadcasts from London, brought new depths to television. His weekly CBS documentary of history was *See It Now*, during which historical characters would stop to "explain" to the camera the significance of the event. Later Murrow in a broadcast was the catalyst for helping to tumble Senator Joseph McCarthy from power after his witch-hunting brought injury to innocent people.

Until the late 1950s, home television reception was exclusively in black-and-white. Then RCA and its NBC network pioneered the introduction of color broadcasting accompanied by color TV sets. The other networks and manufacturers of television sets quickly followed. A side effect of this transition was that every motion picture producer turned to color filming because TV stations would eventually be airing their products.

TV news came into its own increasingly, and importantly it could show news at the moment it happened as it did with Jack Ruby shooting Lee Harvey Oswald in 1963. Virtually every television station had its evening broadcast which competed with rivals and forced many daily newspapers to quit business as subscribers deserted them.

The authorization for Ultra High Frequency (UHF) allowing for channels 14 through 83 encouraged more diversity, particularly after a law requiring all TV sets manufactured after 1964 would receive all signals.

One problem with UHF broadcasts was adjusting the dial to receive the signal properly. Engineers solved this problem in the late 1960s with numbered buttons to call up a channel, and this was refined to the palm-sized wireless box which allowed viewers to control a set from an easy chair.

a popular radio show. The humorist backed Franklin Roosevelt for President in 1932, and received credit for helping him win by a landslide. Rogers was killed in 1935 when the airplane he and Wiley Post were flying crashed in Alaska. In 1952, Route 66 was named the Will Rogers Highway.

The massive Will Rogers Hotel, opened in 1930, at the intersection of Will Rogers Avenue and Route 66 honors his name. One block further west the highway is intersected by Patti Page Avenue, named for the singer who was born in Claremore.

In Tulsa, 11th Street was once an important part of Route 66. Present-day motorists can see numerous vintage motels, some out of business, and others still operating even though antiquated.

Interstate 44, the Turner Turnpike, stretches almost as straight as an arrow from Tulsa to Oklahoma City, but the stretch of former Route 66 between these points is one of the most beautiful sections of the highway. The author noted its charm when there was no turnpike, and over the years has taken the extra time required to travel over Old 66. It is as beautiful as ever, and the

only changes over the years have been the additions of Kmarts, Wal-Marts, and the customary fast food outlets. The countryside is verdant, there are rolling hills shaded by a variety of trees, and the people and livestock are friendly. The author noted four horses drinking water from a pond on Route 66 near Depue and pulled over to make a photograph of this pastoral scene. Almost as soon as he stopped, the horses trotted over to the roadside fence to greet the visitor. The area was green, and friendly people waved to see an out-of-state automobile.

Among the liveliest towns on this stretch of the highway is Sapulpa, a beautiful place with stores that attracted shoppers from the surrounding farms and ranches. A popular stop on Route 66,

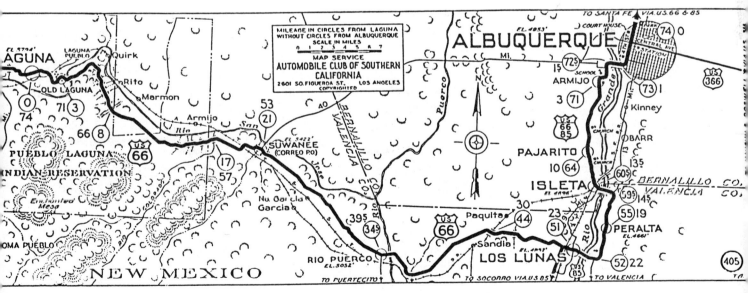

A storm had dumped snow on Clines Corner, then consisting of a gasoline station and small store when this photograph was made in the early 1930s. (Courtesy Sharon Cline McClain)

the city offered numerous motels and restaurants serving truckers and tourists. Even though the interstate passed, it is still lively and, in its old age, graceful. Of interest is the engine house of the Tulsa-Sapulpa Union Railway, an electric interurban line completed in 1918 between its two namesake cities. Despite townspeople's hopes, the railroad never reached Oklahoma City and the lack of patronage caused it to quit carrying passengers in 1943.

Sapulpa is also the home of the Frankoma Pottery Plant, established there in 1938 by the late John Frank and his wife, Grace. Their family still operates the facility, where one can purchase a

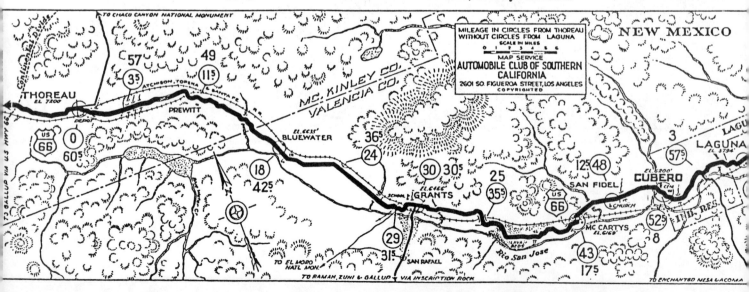

This sign beckoned Route 66 travellers to Clines Corner in the early 1930s. (Courtesy Sharon Cline McClain) BELOW: Now a massive oasis of gift shops, dining facilities, and service stations, Clines Corner stands at the junction of Interstate 40 and the highway to Santa Fe. (Photograph by the Author)

This motel at Moriarty attracted travellers with its "magic" Route 66 sign. (Photograph by the Author)

variety of collectible pottery creations.

In the 1930s, Route 66 truly became the place over which to head West — or East, if that were the case. Gas stations, motels, and restaurants beckoned tourists to stop with a variety of attractions, including souvenirs, live animals, exhibits of cactus, Indian and cowboy apparel, semi-precious rocks, museums, and false fronts for use in snapshots. Some people called them tourist "traps," but families loved them. And stopping at these "traps" provided an excuse to rest, enjoy ice cold soda pop, and gab with other travellers.

Not only the Depression but also crime marked the early 1930s. This was not the drive-by-shooting crime that distinguished the late 20th century in many crowded cities, but groups of individuals, flamboyant in their actions, who often became bigger than life because of newspaper headlines and motion pictures. The Chicago mobsters of the 1920s were organized and methodical in peddling bootleg booze and killing competitors or others who got in the way of rackets which netted them millions of dollars a year. The crooks of the 1930s robbed and killed randomly and without reason.

The epitome of this breed of murderers was John Herbert Dillinger, born in Indianapolis in 1902, and sentenced to jail in 1924 for attempting

An early 1930s photograph showed La Bajada Hill, with 23 hair-pin curves, near Santa Fe.

to rob a bank. When he was released nine years later, he promptly pulled more holdups, was caught, and incarcerated in the jail at Lima, Ohio. Ten fellow criminals descended on the jail, freeing Dillinger and killing the sheriff. Using stolen cars, he then terrorized the Midwest by robbing banks and other establishments, needlessly killing 14 people. To evade detection, he even had plastic surgery to change his looks.

Labeled "Public Enemy No. 1," Dillinger's career ended on July 22, 1934, when FBI agent Melvin Purvis, 31, killed him at the Biograph Theater in Chicago. A mysterious "woman in red" lured him to the theater after law enforcement officers promised that as a reward they would not deport her to her native Romania. He was 32 years old and had spent a third of his life in prison or running from police officers. The mysterious woman was identified as Ann Sage, who was deported after officers broke their word to her.

Another mystery developed; insiders claimed that Ms. Sage was misled, and because of Dillinger's plastic surgery, she fingered the wrong man and the real public enemy went into retirement. They also said the FBI backed off an investigation into the authenticity of his identity because if he indeed was the wrong man the agency could not take credit for the headline-grabbing

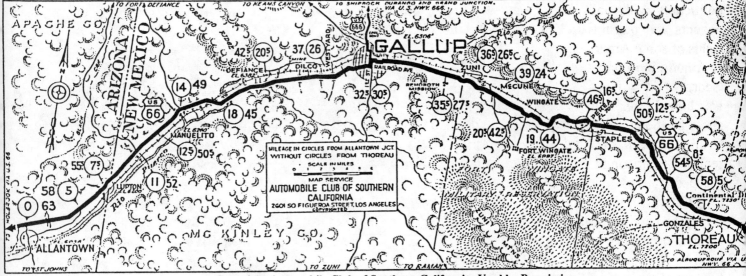

case which fascinated the country.

Melvin Purvis, who apparently clashed with his boss, J. Edgar Hoover, left the agency a year later.

The pursuit of Dillinger and other high-profile criminals made J. Edgar Hoover a public hero. Born in 1895, Hoover became the first director of the Federal Bureau of Investigation in 1924 and held the office until he died in 1972.

In the 1935 motion picture *G-Men*, James Cag-ney, one of the era's most talented actors, portrayed an agent of the Federal Bureau of Investigation and popularized that service, much to the pleasure of J. Edgar Hoover. Idolized by the press and motion pictures, Hoover relentlessly went after felons during the 1930s and during World War II pursued spies. The life-long bachelor seemingly had an unblemished career and was beyond criticism. After his death, reports

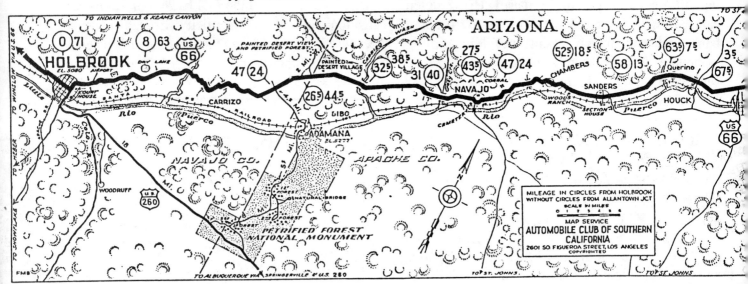

surfaced showing that he provided some politicians with unfavorable data on their opponents and permitted agents to abuse the civil rights of some Americans.

Among the other desperadoes of the time was George "Baby Face" Nelson (1908-1934), who was born Lester Gillis but changed his name because he thought it sounded "sissy." Confined for stealing a car in 1922, he was paroled in 1924 but returned to prison in 1931 for robbing a bank. He escaped from prison soon after arriving there and joined the Dillinger mob. When FBI agents finally engaged and mortally wounded him, he asked a companion to take over and drive because he had been hit by a bullet. In fact, 17 bullets hit him and he died of the wounds. Searching his car, officers found a shotgun and three automatic rifles.

Others who terrorized the Midwest were Bonnie Parker, Clyde Barrow, "Pretty Boy" Floyd, and Ma Barker. Most of their loot, which eventually cost them their lives, was from a few hundred dollars to a hundred thousand dollars, which was a tough way to earn a living. Their compensation was far less that the Chicago bootleggers of the 1920s or the saving and loans executives of the 1980s.

Ma Barker (1871-1935) never personally made it to the Public Enemy No. 1 list, but her activities sounded like a made-for-television movie. Born Arizona Clark near Springfield, Missouri, she changed her name to Kate. A highlight of her childhood was seeing bandit Jesse James in per-

son. She and her husband had four sons, Herman (1894-1927), Arthur (1899-1939), and Fred (1902-1938), three of whom were killed in various brushes with the law. The fourth son, Lloyd Barker (1896-1947) was sent to prison and got out in 1947; he was shot almost immediately by his wife after an argument. Ma Barker worked out details of the bank robberies which they executed, and died in Florida firing machine gun bullets at FBI agents led by Melvin Purvis, who shot Dillinger.

In these chases of the 1930s, by the way, law enforcement officers had to pursue the gangsters on foot or in an automobile. Helicopters, so familiar in the pursuits of criminals, were not yet invented.

Purvis also figured in the conviction of Roger Touhy (1902-1959), who once dominated bootlegging in Des Plains, Illinois. A judge released him from prison in 1959 after determining that indeed the alleged victim had never been kidnapped. He was mysteriously slain a few weeks later. Melvin Purvis shortly thereafter committed suicide.

None other than J. Edgar Hoover in 1936 captured Alvin Karpis, one-time member of the Ma Barker gang. After 33 years in prison, part of it on Alcatraz Island in San Francisco Bay, was released. He wrote his memoirs and retired to Spain where he died.

Despite the crimes these murderers committed, the public seemed fascinated with them. Perhaps

When Route 66 headed north to Santa Fe, one point of interest there was San Miguel Church, believed to have been built in 1541 and possibly the oldest church in America.

this infatuation stemmed from the fact that many victims were banks, generally in bad repute because they wanted to collect loans made to farmers and were reluctant to make more loans without great security because of the Depression. Nevertheless, these men killed many innocent people without any reason whatsoever.

John Steinbeck, in his classic novel of the impoverished Oklahoma farmers, *The Grapes of Wrath*, has a character comment on his people's reluctance to help catch outlaws.

Perhaps because they personally did not see the terror or brutality of these killers, the public was fascinated with them — not just at that time but in years to come. Hollywood made at least three movies about Dillinger (1945, 1973, 1991), plus *The Story of Pretty Boy Floyd*, (1974) with Martin Sheen as Floyd; *The Bonnie Parker Story* (1958) in which Dorothy Provine played Ms. Parker; *Bonnie and Clyde*, (1967) with Warren Beatty and Faye Dunaway in the title roles; *Ma Barker's Killer Brood* (1960), with Lurene Tuttle playing the lady gangster, and Mickey Rooney as *Baby Face Nelson*. The ruthless dean of criminals was portrayed by Rod Steiger in *Al Capone* (1959).

The Great Depression raged on, with millions of workers still unemployed. Yet the people saw hope ahead with the WPA which put idle people to work, not just building Route 66 but also creating art, erecting public buildings, writing history and plays, performing in stage productions, and repairing public buildings.

In 1936, despite opposition from eighty percent of the nation's daily newspapers, Franklin Roosevelt overwhelmingly was reelected president, receiving 523 electoral votes to the only 8 that went to his Republican opponent, Alfred Landon of Kansas.

Until then no American president had ever served more than two terms. With the Depression still a problem and Americans against entering the European war which started in 1939, voters reelected Roosevelt for an unprecedented third term. By 1944, with the United States in the war, voters returned him for a fourth term.

Back on Route 66 heading south in Oklahoma toward Texas, the road passes abandoned motels and service stations. The community of Texola

This early 1940s view showed a road in northern New Mexico which became accessible when Route 66 opened. BELOW: A Native American woman weaves a blanket as a train rolls by. The Santa Fe paralleled Route 66 through much of New Mexico and in Arizona and California.

A 1930s scene showed Albuquerque's Central Avenue when it was the city's main shopping district. BELOW: Here is a 1990s view of the same scene. Walgreen's replaced Woolworth's, the bank building is still there, some stores are vacant, and the street is blocked for redevelopment. (Photograph by the Author)

Route 66 Grew Up

Western America was emerging from its infancy when Route 66 came into being. When people in the East referred to the West, "Out West" was Chicago. California was the "Far West." Advertisements for many products often carried the footnote, "Prices Slightly Higher West of the Rockies" because production was concentrated in the East, home for most of the nation's people.

With its attractions, California was growing as a vacation area. The unreliability automobiles and lack of mechanical services after one left a city made long-distance travel, except by train, a problem. Most people therefore travelled by rail: there were four lines: the Santa Fe, Southern Pacific, Western Pacific, and Union Pacific, each running several passenger trains daily between Chicago and the West Coast.

All of that changed with the coming of Route 66.

Chicago, the city by the lake from which Route 66 started, was a manufacturing, rail, and trading center which was second in America only to New York City during the 1920s. When Route 66 closed in 1984, Los Angeles had overtaken Chicago and was America's second city and a major manufacturing center.

In the 1920s, there were fewer slums in the large cities and American society was socially friendlier and had less class divisions. When Route 66 ended, both Chicago and Los Angeles unfortunately had more slums and more crime areas than when Route 66 began. There was also a greater difference in income and living standards between the people throughout America.

Thanks to technology and people's literacy, almost every town of 10,000 or more had a daily newspaper in the 1920s. Some boasted two, one Democratic and the other Republican. Los Angeles boasted six dailies, plus one or two daily newspapers in 15 or more satellite cities. By the 1980s newspapers were beginning to fold under the pressure of declining reading skills and the competition from radio, television, and other newspapers.

Until electric refrigerators triumphed in the 1940s, almost every city had at least one ice company that sent refrigerated trucks through the neighborhoods.

A prehistoric "monster" adds color and "guards" the entrance to the Grand Canyon Caverns at Peach Tree, Between Seligman and Kingman. One reaches the attraction by leaving Interstate 40.

Responding to square signs in residential windows identifying the preferred company, the ice man carried blocks of the product in a leather bag over his shoulder through the backdoor to the wooden refrigerator, which was insulated to keep the ice for a few days. These refrigerators would not keep ice cream.

Schools were very much like modern ones except students lacked ballpoint pens. They obtained ink from a desk's glass well which a janitor refilled each night. Ballpoint pens came along in 1947 and initially commanded a price of $15, almost as much as the average worker received daily, because they were so

Back in Route 66 days, Canyon Lodge at the site of Two Guns in the 1930s offered travelers rooms, cottages, supplies, and even free space for camping. In the early 20th century Two Guns was a roaring settlement of saloons and brothels. (Courtesy of *Route 66 Magazine*)

novel.

Arrivals to Southern California were greeted by clear blue skies and sunshine almost every day of the year, at least until the coming of smog in the early 1950s. Alongside Route 66 were forests of orange and lemon trees, plus pleasant vineyards. If tourists tired of driving, there was the 1,100-mile Pacific Electric trolley system stretching from Mission San Fernando through Los Angeles to Redlands, and from the snow-capped mountains to the ocean.

Instead of improving the aging trolley system, Southern California replaced it with lackluster freeways and when these proved inadequate started a new rail transit system — putting part of it through sandy soil which would move when jolted by the "big one" predicted by earthquake expert Charles Richter.

Smog, the pollution of air by manufacturers and cars, also was ignored despite warnings by scientists that it would cut short people's lives.

Many traditions changed with the concurrent arrival of shopping malls and television, automatic washers and dryers, and other appliances in the late 1940s. Virtually all mall stores remained open until daily 9 p.m. or 10 p.m., and until 6 p.m. on Sundays. Downtown merchants — if lucky enough to remain in business — were forced to adopt those hours.

Until the coming of the malls, central Los Angeles was the place to shop, even though several surrounding cities boasted small "downtowns."

"The City," as residents called Los Angeles, had several quality department stores. Among them were The Broadway, Bullock's, J.J. Haggerty's (later renamed Robinson's), and the May Company, none of which had branches outside of Los Angeles proper until well into the 1950s. Each was full-service, offering everything from toys and clothing to radios and

Still welcoming tourists, Two Guns is reached by way of Exit 330 on Interstate 40. There modern-day travellers can see the remnants of the lusty town where early-day cowpokes lived and died. Two Guns is east of Flagstaff. (Courtesy of *Route 66 Magazine*)

furniture.

The family saved money or used a bank to buy a home or other purchases. In 1958 California-based Bank of America changed all of this by introducing what it called the BankAmericard, the grandparent of the Visa Card and Master Card. Eager for new gadgets without saving for them, families bought things immediately. Many households found themselves on a merry-go-round of charging and spending at 18 percent or more interest annually. Housewives were forced to work to help make the payments.

Until 1940, Los Angeles area residents made their livings as the result of money generated by orange groves, vineyards, the motion picture industry, and expenditures of retirees and tourists. World War II brought aircraft plants, shipyards, assorted industries, and hordes of new people. Smog and hordes of new residents followed.

In the late 1940s I was a writer for the All-Year Club of Southern California, whose announced goal was to bring more visitors to the area. Its community-based backers hoped, however, to lure more residents to boost the value of real estate and businesses. My job was to write stories about the region's attractions, which I loved and still love. It was an easy, leisurely job with a friendly boss, Alan McElwain, who would be my friend for decades.

After determining the All-Year Club's unannounced goal, I resigned. My fears came true in a few years: the orange trees and other agricultural developments gave way to carbon-copy home tracts and look-alike shopping malls.

Those who profited were the wealthy owners of stores, newspapers, acreage, and automobile agencies.

Settlements that once were villages became cities with boundaries lapping against each other like jig-

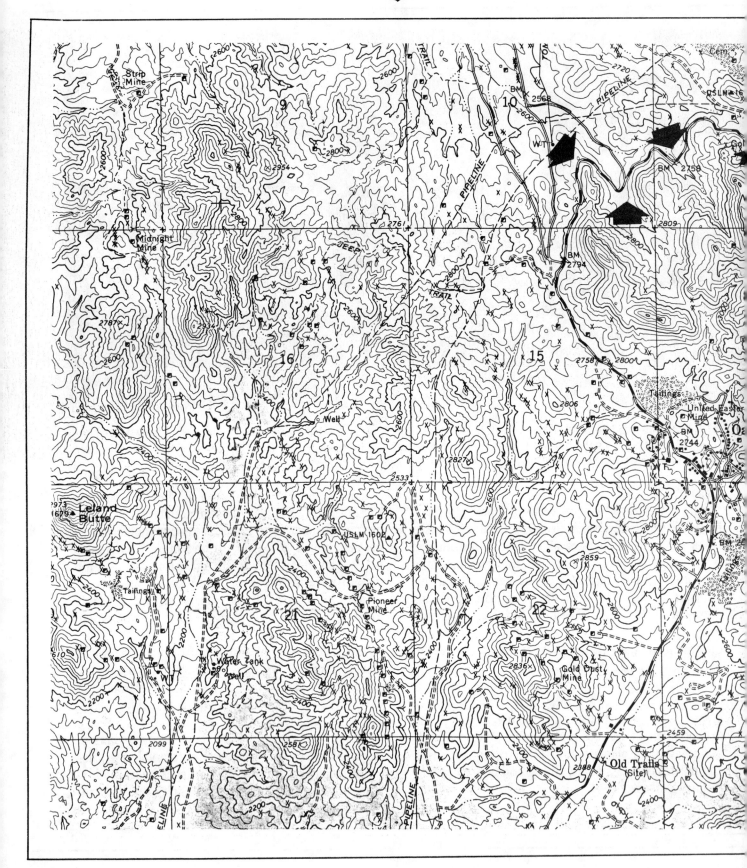

Here is the main street of Oatman, a lively ghost towm and mining center, which was on Old Route 66. LEFT: This topographic map shows the winding road (arrows) through Sitgreave Pass, just east of Oatman. Its steep grades caused engines to overheat in the 1920s until Interstate 40 bypassed the artery.

saw puzzles so that a person could not tell where one city ended and another began.

The logical solution, at least for efficiency and taxpayer savings, would be to merge all cities and other political subdivisions into one unit. It could be called, appropriately, the City of Southern California. Police, fire, and other agencies would be centralized, eliminating waste.

The only losers would be members of city councils, school boards and other repetitious bureaucracies.

When Route 66 ended in 1984, health and many other important things had improved, but those residing at the the western and eastern end of old Highway 66 still sought to solve social and economic problems that came with the growth.

General Omar Bradley had this to say in 1959:

"If we are not careful, we shall leave our children a legacy of billion-dollar roads leading nowhere except to other congested places like those they left behind. We are building ourselves an asphalt treadmill and allowing the green areas of our nation to disappear."

By the time Route 66 ended, the lifestyles of America had changed in many ways.

The pleasures of dances, proms, week-end outings, the first look at a new-born child, kids' birthday parties, and love remained unchanged.

H-1854 HOTEL CASTANEDA, LAS VEGAS, N. M.

ABOVE: Modeled after a California mission, the Hotel Castaneda in Las Vegas, New Mexico, served travelers when Route 66 in its early days went through the city. **BELOW:** Amarillo's downtown Polk Street in 1939 boasted it was the "best lighted" main street in America. Copyright McCormick Company; used with permission.

The Best Lighted "Main Street" in America

Polk Street, Amarillo, Texas, Looking North from Ninth   © 1939, MC CORMICK CO., AMARILLO—PHOTO 3351

This scene was farther west on Central Avenue during the 1930s. The ornate Kimo Theater, at the left, still stands. BELOW: The Route 66 Restaurant, also on Central Avenue, was erected where a Phillips 66 service station once stood. (Photograph by the Author)

stands almost on the border of Texas and Oklahoma, but the post office is in the latter state. The city of Shamrock is a jolly place that radiates

Shops vending Route 66 souvenirs are up and down the highway. This one is on Central Avenue in Albuquerque. (Photo by the Author)

charm and fun. Every year the townspeople stage a celebration, on Saint Patrick's Day, March 17, and the city is even more jovial. Shamrock's main street is graced with a park in a setting where the walls of surrounding buildings are decorated with scenes that one might see in an Irish village. The art decco tower of a one-time Conoco service station with an adjoining restaurant is still impressive. Early-day motels, some still operating, await visitors on Route 66. Heading West, Old Route 66 went through McLean, today still a busy and picturesque town.

In Amarillo one of the larger cities in Texas, Route 66 entered on Amarillo Boulevard, turned down Fillmore, and exited the city on Sixth Street. Several early-day motels remain, some in varying stages of disrepair and others maintained and still operating. Interstate 40 crosses the city north of Old Route 66, with many modern motels now on each side of it. The Inn of the Big Texan, once situated on "66" moved with its restaurant, souvenir shop, and lodging facilities to an I-40 service road east of the city. It advertises for miles in each direction that the patron who consumes a 72-pound steak, plus side dishes, in an hour or less can have it free. Few diners take the challenge, but some do and win at the game. Palo Duro Canyon, a breathtaking sight, is a few minutes south of Amarillo.

Heading west from Amarillo is the Cadillac Ranch, an attraction with 10 of the famous tail-finned-Cadillacs built from 1948 to 1964 and the pride of the owner, Stanley Marsh 3. The automobiles are buried, rear ends up, in cement. An open gate and path lead to the cars from the service road, once part of "66."

Yellow and red signs appear periodically along the highway for miles proclaiming, "Tucumcari

This mural on a building on Albuquerque's Central Avenue depicts the westward movement from the covered wagon era to the present. BELOW: This motel on Central Avenue expresses the pride of being on Route 66. (Photograph by the Author)

This is a 1930s view of the Sky City of Acoma, built on a mesa 300 feet above the surrounding plain. BELOW: This is San Esteban Mission, established in 1629 by the Spaniards at Acoma.

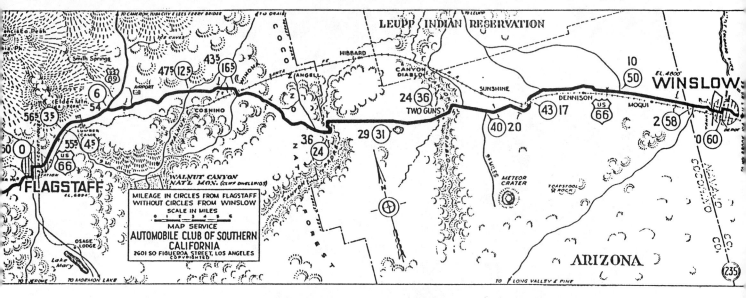

Tonight," and urging motorists to push on a bit further. Soon, after crossing into New Mexico, the motorist arrives in the town that has clung to its reputation as a good place to eat and sleep through the years. While there are several new hotels and the standard franchised restaurants, many vintage motels and cafes in reasonably good condition remain in operation along with vacant ones that failed when the interstate came.

Further west is Santa Rosa, in Route 66 days a town that thrived on tourists and truckers.

Numerous "66" era motels and gas stations, along with new ones, remain in operation, but the residents, many of them friendly, helpful people of Spanish ancestry shake their heads when they speak of the days before the interstate forced many restaurants and other businesses to close.

Why don't they move to larger communities with better opportunities? Santa Rosa, like many other Route 66 towns, is a relatively crime-free place where the residents know, trust, and help each other. They fear that moving, and probably

This is the pueblo of Cubero on Old Route 66 south of Grants. Little has changed over the years except for the addition of modern signs. (Photograph by the Author)

A 1940s photograph showed Route 66 heading through Native American reservations near Grants. Mount Taylor, named for President Zachary Taylor, rises in the background. BELOW: A "gag" postcard popular during the 1930s appeared in many versions and poked fun at boastful Westerners by showing a cowboy aboard a jack rabbit. No, Folks, the rabbit really wasn't that big!

TX-5   Texas Cowboy Riding a Jack Rabbit

CONTINENTAL
DIVIDE

ELEVATION 7,263 FEET

Rainfall divides at this
point. To the west it
drains into the Pacific
Ocean—to the east,
into the Atlantic.

Route 66 crossed the Continental Divide approximately 115 miles west of Albuquerque and 30 miles east of Gallup. From this divide, creeks, streams, and rivers run east or west. The divide stretches from Alaska to the American Southwest.

rightfully so, would put them in an environment of strangers, dense traffic, and gangs.

Even though a generation has grown up since the interstate came into being, Route 66 perpetuates itself in remaining stretches of the highway and in public interest. "Historic Route 66" signs hang in shop windows or are attached to lamp posts and other fixtures along the stretch from Chicago to L.A. Driving westward on Old "66" toward Moriarty, a motorist coming from the other direction hailed the author and, in Spanish, asks if there is a dead-end ahead or can he continue on "seis-seis" without turning about. Assured there is a way out, he smiles and proceeds.

Route 66 is famed internationally.

Many towns have their "Route 66" plazas, restaurants, motels, and souvenir shops. As if they know there are appreciative visitors listening, radio stations broadcast renditions of Bobby Troup's *Get Your Kicks on Route 66*.

It is almost as though one is in a time warp, and the calendar has been turned back to the 1930s or 1940s. Cruising along, away from cities, a motorist can receive only a few radio stations. Many broadcast the distinctive music of the 1930s and 1940s, adding to the feeling of bygone decades.

When Route 66 reached Albuquerque, it went

Owl Rock on Highway 66 between Grants and Albuquerque

Owl Rock was a landmark between Grants and Albuquerque on Route 66, which was just two lanes wide at this point in the 1930s. BELOW LEFT: A 1930s photograph showed Native Americans by a hogan, the multi-sided dwelling built by tribes. RIGHT: Steep grades and warm weather combined to make radiator problems on Old Route 66; this shop was in Grants.

Navajo Indians on Reservation

Charlie's RADIATOR SERVICE

This Magnolia station was typical of the smaller gas outlets in the Southwest during the Route 66 era. Magnolia was a predecessor of Mobil. (Mobil Oil Company Archives)

down Central Avenue, which is almost as straight as an arrow. Motels, service stations, and restaurants grew along Central, and in the era before there were shopping malls, it was also Albuquerque's main business and shopping area.

In the glory days of rail travel, many Santa Fe Railroad passenger trains passed through Albuquerque several times a day. Even by 1956 when rail passenger service was declining, *The Official Guide to Railways* listed several trains daily bound from Chicago to Los Angeles. The Santa Fe *Chief* travelled through the city at 7:40 every morning, while *El Capitan* arrived at 2:35 p.m., and trains from Houston and Galveston to Los Angeles went through Albuquerque at 3:55 p.m. and 5:40 p.m. every day. In addition, other schedules from Chicago to Los Angeles brought

trains through Albuquerque at 7:30 a.m., and afternoons at 3:45, 4:50, and 5:15.

Each day, of course, there were corresponding eastern-bound schedules.

The trains stopped for various lengths of time, but always long enough for greetings from the Native Americans who met the travellers. These pow wows gave the passengers the opportunities to see a touch of the West that motorists enjoyed on their trips through New Mexico and Arizona. Wearing their tribal garments, the Native Americans created colorful scenes as they sold pottery, blankets, jewelry, Kachinas, and other hand-made items. With Amtrak, only one passenger train arrives from each direction, but Native Americans still greet the arrivals and peddle their wares.

In the 1930s, Native American culture came alive, probably for the first time, for many tourists journeying West. This 1930 scene showed Indians displaying merchandise at the Santa Fe station in Albuquerque. Motorists also met Native Americans at reservations on and near the highway, as they still do. (Courtesy Santa Fe Railroad)

Old Town, at Rio Grande Boulevard and Old Highway 66, is a marketplace blending the cultures of Spain, Mexico, and Native America — plus a few late arrivals, the Anglo-Americans. If one drives through nearby neighborhoods, a person will see numerous modern cottages built with

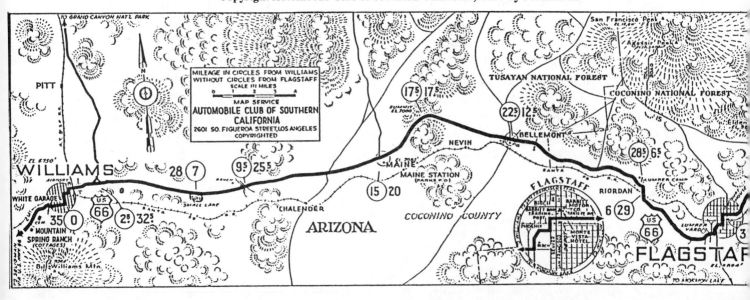

Part of the pleasures of travelling on Route 66 was stopping at the Fred Harvey restaurants and hotels at cities served by the Santa Fe Railroad. One of the most beautiful was the Spanish style La Posada ("The Lodging") at Winslow.

traditional Hispanic and Indian architectural lines, and making a welcome contrast to the box-like tract homes found in so many places. The Spanish Conquistadores started settling New Mexico in 1540, locating in what is now Old Town. Beginning with a traditional plaza with homes, church, and government buildings, the pueblo grew into metropolitan Albuquerque. Route 66 with its tourists and new residents, helped that growth.

Just a mile or so up Rio Grande Boulevard, at Interstate 40 exit 157A, is the Indian Pueblo Cultural Center. Here 19 Native American tribes have united in establishing a museum, center for presenting traditional dances, and shops with Indian and other gifts.

Several tribes reside on reservations or in towns along Route 66. In Oklahoma, there are Indians traditionally associated with the Plains, including the Arapahoe, Cherokee, Cheyenne, Comanche, Creek, Choctaw, Chickasaw, Kiowa,

and Osage tribes. Apache, Navajo, and Zuni tribes live in New Mexico. In northern Arizona, there are Apaches, Hopis, Navajos, and Yavapais, many of whom wreak out bare subsistences on the land. In driving over the countryside, one often sees television antennas and even TV saucers, and cannot help but wonder how these people assess living in big cities as compared to their outdoor environment.

Each tribe has its own designs for pottery, blankets, jewelry, and other crafts.

While motoring on Old Route 66 over the countryside, travellers scanning a radio will hear Native American broadcasting stations using native languages to give news or introduce music, much of it of Indian origin. The only hint that this is the United States may come when an advertising announcement is punctuated with the name "Wal-Mart," "Kmart," or some other store seeking patronage from the tribes. In World War II,

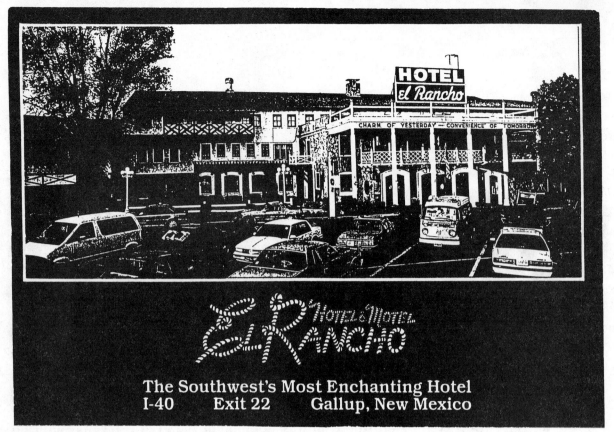

The Southwest's Most Enchanting Hotel
I-40   Exit 22   Gallup, New Mexico

El Rancho Hotel and Motel in Gallup, built on Route 66 during the mid-1930s, has been renovated and with its photographs of motion picture and other celebrity guests, attracts visitors. While Native Americans of the area built multi-sided hogans for dwellings, many trading posts erect teepees because travellers expect to see them. These teepees are in the northern section of Gallup.

Route 66 on TV

Many people regard the 1950s and early 1960s as the Golden Age of Television. In a new medium, here were imaginative programs: *I Love Lucy, The Milton Berle Show, The Honeymooners,* and on the dramatic side, *Gunsmoke, Perry Mason, The Twilight Zone, The Hallmark Theater,* and far from the least, *Route 66.*

Debuting in 1960, *Route 66* had high ratings but went off in 1964. As a cult favorite it is still seen on late nights over TV stations in many cities.

Creators of the series were Stirling Silliphant, who received an Academy Award for writing *In the Heat of the Night,* and Herbert Leonard. In the series, two young men cruised Route 66 in a Corvette, having adventures in several locales. While the stories revolved around "66," the actual locations were often in other parts of America in order to have good filming weather and different settings.

The stars were Martin Milner, who made his screen debut in the 1947 film *Life with Father* and also was featured in the TV series *Adams 12,* and George Maharis, who went on for a career in theatrical motion pictures. When Maharis became ill, actor Glenn Corbett took over the role.

Martin Milner and George Maharis (below) were the stars in the 1960s television series *Route 66*. When Maharis became ill, Glenn Corbett assumed his role.

Pleased with the exposure, Chevrolet provided the series with a new Corvette every year.

The obvious theme for the series would have been Bobby Troup's *Get Your Kicks on Route 66,* but the producers avoided paying him royalty by having composer Nelson Riddle write the music.

Guests, some of them in the early stages of their careers, took roles in various episodes of the series. Among the Academy Award winners to be who appeared were Robert Duvall, Gene Hackman, Lee Marvin, Robert Redford, and Rod Steiger.

Other guest stars included Alan Alda, Ed Asner, Cloris Leachman, and Jean Stapleton.

The series was dubbed in six languages, and helped acquaint many overseas viewers with the legendary Route 66 which was tucked away in the southwestern portion of the United States.

A photograph from the early days of Route 66 showed Kitchen's Opera House on Route 66 between Second and Third Streets in Gallup. At the right is the Eagle Cafe, which in the 1990s was still in business. (Sally Noe Collection)

Navajos with the U.S. forces used their native language for two-way radio messages with the knowledge that they would not be understandable to the Germans or Japanese.

Western residents understand the profiles of the people who live in northern New Mexico and Arizona, but visitors from the east lack that knowledge. There is a combination of Hispanic, Native American, and Anglo American culture reflected in the architecture, speech, food, and garb, all existing together with varying amounts of understanding and appreciation.

Heading west from Albuquerque, Route 66 led travellers into beautiful, primitive country with Indian reservations and trading posts. Motorists can leave Interstate 40 and drive over Old Route 66 through the Indian pueblos of Laguna and Cubero. In the city of Grants, Route 66 took the name of Santa Fe Avenue, where motels and other tourist facilities grew and remain. Once the center of uranium mining, the city has the New Mexico Mining Museum. South of the highway is Acoma Sky Pueblo, a mesa towering 300 feet above the plain. The ancient Native Americans chose the top of the rock for their pueblo because it afforded protection from invaders. From the top, visitors can look down on another mesa with a similar city, abandoned centuries ago.

The Plains Indians used teepees, the inverted "V"-shaped shelters of buffalo skins, and along

Drake Hotel
Gallup N. Mex.

A 1920s scene in Gallup on Route 66 and Strong Street shows the upstairs Drake Hotel, which still stands. Note the curb-side gasoline pump and headquarters for the stage to Farmington, a 140-mile trip that required two days. (Sally Noe Collection)

Route 66 one finds many such structures built of hides, plyboard, plastic, or burlap. These teepees were erected to entertain and attract tourists, in may cases by wily Native Americans who know what visitors expect. The Indians of northern New Mexico and Arizona lived in cliff dwellings, adobe houses, or hogans, which are octagon-shaped structures made with tree trunks. Those dwellings are much less spectacular than the teepees of the Plains, so the merchants recognize that there is no business like show business and they build teepees.

Gallup, long proud of its title as the Indian capital of America, is one of the few smaller cities on Route 66 that has thrived despite being by-passed by Interstate 40. Many souvenir shops, some privately operated and others owned by tribes, sell souvenirs.

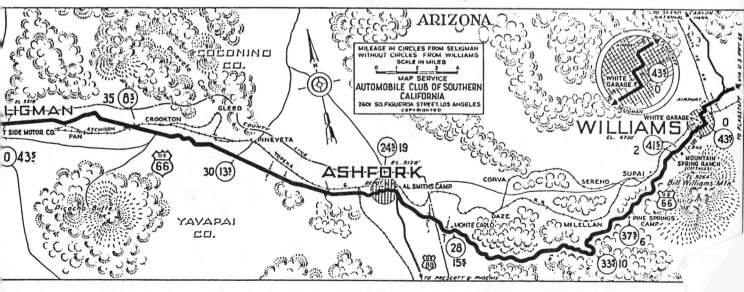

A 1958 photograph on Route 66 at the eastern end of Gallup advised visitors that they were entering "The Indian Capital." (Sally Noe Collection)

At the New Mexico-Arizona border, an assortment of shops vending Native American wares, complete with teepees, has stood on Old Route 66 for decades. Farther on, there is a settlement marked on older maps as the trading post of Courage. This area later became the site of Fort Courage for the *F Troop* television series starring Forest Tucker. The fort built for the production remains (admission charge), along with an example of a hogan into which visitors can enter. Nearby is a different variety of hogan, built with the help of plaster and which shows how Native Americans have adapted their lifestyles to changing times.

While life on Route 66 showed few changes except for new motels and other service facilities, Americans coped with the challenge of surviving during the Great Depression. One diversion was the development of the Technicolor process for producing motion pictures in color. It was introduced in a 1935 short, *La Cucaracha*, starring Don Alvarado and Steffi Duna. The first Technicolor feature production, also made in 1935, was *Becky Sharp*, with Miriam Hopkins and Alan Mowbray. While more and more motion pictures using color were made in the ensuing years, it was not until the arrival of color television in the 1960s that black-and-white films were abandoned. There was turmoil in Europe because of economic crises caused in part by high U.S. tariffs resulting in a reduction of imports to the United States and bringing unemployment. Adolf Hitler came to power in Germany in 1933, using the swastika to hail a "new" order. Curiously enough, the Native Americans of New Mexico and Arizona favored that symbol, producing and selling thousands of silver rings, bracelets, necklaces,

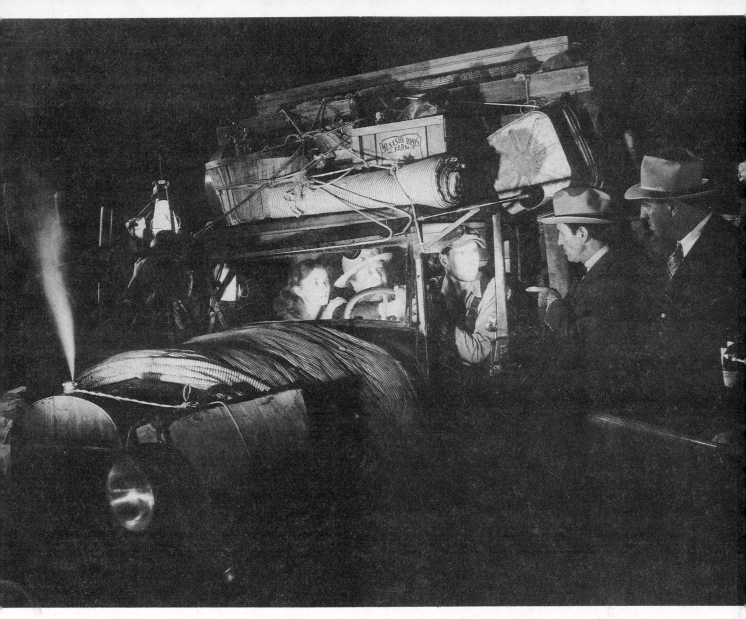

Henry Fonda, portraying Tom Joad in the 1940 film about Oklahoma migrants, *The Grapes of Wrath*, faces an officer, played by Charles Middleton. Seated by Fonda is Jane Darwell, who portraying Ma Joad won the Academy Award for best supporting actress.

and earrings to tourists. To trading posts easily recognizable to tourists, many painted swastikas on their walls or signs. At the first, many attempted to disassociate themselves from the Germans by noting that the Nazi swastika was right-handed while the one used by the Indians was left-handed. Nazi brutality unfortunately reduced the swastika symbol to one that was abhorred; few people would be caught wearing such a piece of jewelry for fear that they would be mistaken for Hitler sympathizers.

So popular was the swastika during the 1930s that one northern Arizona hostelery was innocently named the Swastika Hotel and placed an advertisement in an automobile club book of maps. When Hitler came to power, the hotel, of course, changed its name.

Over the years the Route 66 area was favored for numerous motion pictures, most of them of the cowboy genre. An exception was the Robert Sherwood play *The Petrified Forest*, which opened in 1935 with Leslie Howard and a new-

Ocotillo plants, which are tall and spiny, grow along Old Route 66 in the deserts of Arizona and California. Ranchers sometimes plant them in rows to form fences.

comer named Humphrey Bogart in the principal roles of the New York City production. When it was time for the motion picture to be made, Howard agreed to play his role only if Bogart could reprise his part because of his professional regard for the actor. Bette Davis also joined the cast. Portraying a gangster, Bogart copied the mannerisms of gangster John Dillinger and became a star overnight. The plot dealt with travellers trapped in the northern Arizona desert by gangsters.

In early 1934, a tragedy occurred that produced a great impact on the Southwest's social structure, and much of the drama centered on Highway 66. Heavy winds blowing across countless acres in Oklahoma and Arkansas carried priceless soil away from farms where the owners and their helpers already suffered from low prices for their crops. The Dust Bowl was formed. In the ensuing months, farmers who owned or leased their land for years lost their property for lack of funds to pay loans or rent. Share-croppers were ousted abruptly by landlords who planned to increase profits by industrialization using farm machinery.

Farming corporations in California's San Joaquin Valley took advantage of their plight by distributing fliers offering these people work picking grapes, citrus, and other crops. Families hoping for better lives farther west, loaded their family belongings into aging pickups, trucks, and automobiles, many of them barely able to run, and headed over Route 66 to California. The expression applied to the migrants was "Okies," which probably initially was not intended for disparagement but to identify them by accents with which people were not familiar. In fact, then and now people in the state refer to their capitol, Oklahoma City, as "OK City" for brevity. The word "Okie" often was applied to migrants or other people from elsewhere with similar accents who migrated and struggled to find new lives.

When the farm people reached California, they

Buses also cruised Route 66, carrying passengers from Chicago to Santa Monica and points in between. Most of them were the Greyhound Lines or Santa Fe Trailways, but there also were assorted tour and private buses. This mural on a wall in Kingman was painted as a salute to them.

learned that the fliers misrepresented their pay, which proved to be half or less of what the advertisements offered. In addition, many migrants were denied their civil rights, sometimes by California officers who attempted to keep them from entering the state and later by company or county officers. The federal government estab-

lished camps where the people could stay while they sorted out their lives and sought jobs. While this did not solve the problem, it provided direly needed relief for the poverty-stricken travellers.

John Steinbeck's best-selling novel, *The Grapes of Wrath*, in graphic terms told of the struggle, describing the trek on Route 66 on nar-

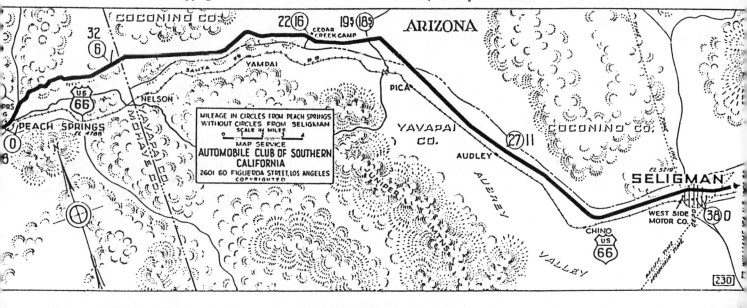

An automobile travels the cutoff to the Petrified Forest and Painted Desert from Route 66 east of Holbrook. BELOW: Here is a 1930s photograph of the marvelous forest of "stone" trees.

678   DRIFT LOGS IN SECOND FOREST, PETRIFIED FOREST, ARIZONA

6A-H1508

This is the set built for the *F Troop* television series at the trading post at Courage. In front is a hogan built of wood which visitors can inspect. BELOW: Adjoining the fort is a different kind of hogan. It follows Indian architectural lines but uses plaster and a composition roof. (Both Photographs by the Author)

row or steep roads, dilapidated vehicles, cruel weather, and sometimes the crueler words spat at them by onlookers who did not understand them. Director John Ford in 1940 made the book into a masterpiece film in which Henry Fonda gave one of his best performances of his career. The motion picture was made on Route 66 in Oklahoma, near the Colorado River near Topock, and at a government camp for migrants at Pomona.

The Oklahomans' journey of Route 66 was a difficult one. They had little money to buy gas, even at bargain prices as low as 12 cents a gallon, or for food to feed their families. Accounts show that the owners and employees of stores, gas stations, and restaurants along the way exercised compassion. Some store owners loaned small amounts of money that eventually were repaid, and others made outright gifts of food, gas, and money. The Oklahomans, who were proud individuals, stopped to work for as little as $1.00 a day on farms or at cleaning tasks in order to get money to move on. They often camped at wide places beside the highway or in clearings in the forests or deserts. These migrants were not beg-

ARIZONA
US
66

gars, but hard workers and responsible people who were down on their luck and sought new opportunities. All of the business people along the way were not brutal, as demonstrated in a scene from John Ford's film where a cashier in a store reduces the price of a candy bar to almost nothing for a child. A letter in a 1992 issue of *Roadsigns*, the newsletter of the California Route 66 Association, told how a mechanic along the way repaired the family automobile, explaining they never knew what the problem was because he did not charge them.

As a youngster on a trip through Arizona at the time, the author recalls seeing a woman with five small children hitchhiking beside a road in a tiny, desolate town. He watched as the kids waved; the oldest child, a girl probably 13 years old, also smiled and curtsied to us. To this day he wonders what kind person with a vehicle large enough for the family finally stopped to help them, and if those youngsters found the security and happiness they deserved.

In Oklahoma and parts of Texas there were trees to shade the travellers at many points, as there were around Flagstaff and Williams. The elevations ranged from 6,894 feet at Flagstaff to 5,219 feet at Seligman, with these altitudes often giving some moderate, enjoyable temperatures. One of the most precarious stretches of Route 66 is between Kingman and Oatman, where the highway winds over Sitgreave's Pass.

Down in the desert the temperatures are warm in general and scorching during the summers. The Oklahomans who made the trip during the summer could expect the thermometer to soar to 110 degrees or more. Automobiles in that era lacked the power or cooling systems that came in later years, and radiators boiled and even blew up going up hills in the desert heat. The migrants, as well as other motorists, carried cans and canvas bags filled with water to give drinks to their thirsty radiators. Every service station brought the

For decades signs of a giant jack rabbit aroused curiosity for miles up and down Route 66. BELOW: Here's what tourists see, as did thousands before them, when they get to the Jack Rabbit Trading Post at Joseph City. (Photographs by the Author)

The Wigwam Motel has been a landmark at Holbrook for decades. (Courtesy Elinor Cole: Wigwam Motel) BELOW LEFT: Here is the way the motel, with units actually shaped like teepees, looked in the 1990s. RIGHT: This is the Old West Museum in Holbrook. (Both Photographs by the Author)

Approximately 10 miles south of Old Highway 66 between Winslow and Two Guns is Meteor Crater, formed thousands of years ago when an immense meteor fell to earth. BELOW: Visitors view the meteor, which is a mile across and 800 feet deep. (Both Photographs © Meteor Crater Enterprises; used by permission)

feeling of relief that here was more water. If the travellers had enough change, they would buy soda pop, especially for the kids. When the highway finally reached Barstow, the motorists turned from Route 66 to the road to Bakersfield via the town of Mojave. Some stayed in Bakersfield, in the southern section of the vast San Joaquin Valley, to work in the fields. Others moved northward to valley communities such as Arvin, Buttonwillow, Hanford, Lamont, Lindsay, Pixley, Wasco, Porterville, Fraser, Selma, Orange Cove, or Fresno. Here were the citrus orchards, vineyards, and cotton fields. The great disappointment for the migrants was learning the fliers advertising jobs were false, and that their pay would only be a part of what was promised. Some left Route 66 even further behind, travelling up to Sacramento, where the pay for farm work was equally distorted. The aircraft plants in the Los

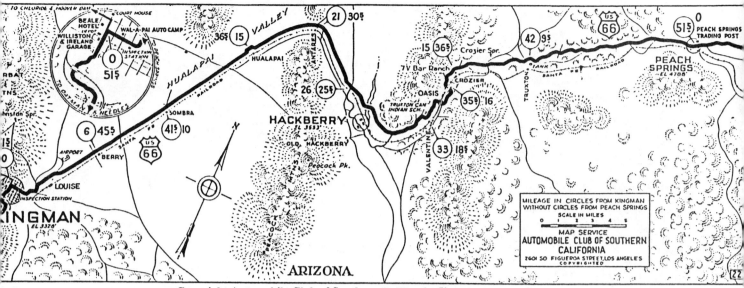

Angeles area, tuning up for what would be World War II, beckoned some migrants.

The children and grandchildren of these migrants remained in the San Joaquin Valley to serve the area as business and professional people.

Motion pictures were a big part of American life in the 1930s and 1940s, when virtually every community had a theater where films shaped social and political life. Although *The Grapes of Wrath* may have dramatized the plight of the Oklahoma migrants it was not the picture that typified the nation at the time. The picture, or rather series, that America believed depicted the average American family was the one revolving the fictional Hardy Family. The initial one, *A Family Affair*, made in 1937, catapulted Mickey Rooney to stardom. The Hardy Family, with

Rooney as son Andy, was also composed of the father, mother, and sister living on the kind of quiet residential street which one might hope to find in any small to medium-sized city along Route 66 or anywhere else in the United States. Actually the family was an upper-middle class one, with a house and amenities much nicer than the average household could afford at the time, but the series gave audiences something for which they could strive and hope as the Hardys met typical family problems with some drama and a great deal of humor. In all the series included 17 motion pictures, three of which co-starred Judy Garland. By 1939 Mickey Rooney was No. 1 at the box office.

Cinema critics define 1939 as the "golden" year when the Hollywood studios produced several films that became classics. They include

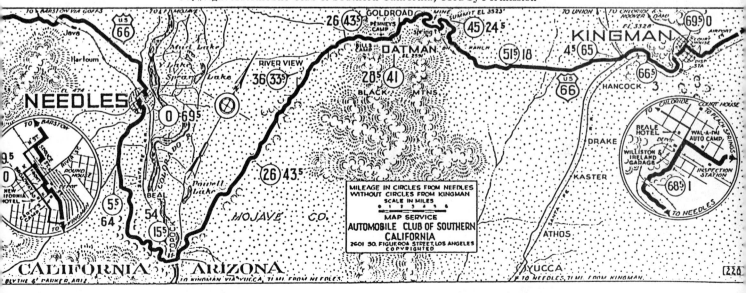

San Francisco Peak rises behind Flagstaff, which had a population of 10,000 in the 1930s, when this photograph probably was made. BELOW: The Twin Arrows Trading Post has been a landmark for years on Route 66. (Photograph by the Author)

Gone with the Wind, The Wizard of Oz, The Great Dictator, Rebecca, Stagecoach, Wuthering *Heights,* and *Goodbye, Mr. Chips.*

American motion pictures in the 1920s through the early 1950s most often were filmed in the Hollywood studios or their southern California ranches, with some "location" scenes in nearby areas for settings that were too specialized for construction on a movie lot. Except for these nearby excursions, the movie makers erected elaborate sets of well-known United States and European streets, palaces, western towns, and other locales. Not until after World War II did the studios make excursions, often highly expensive, to overseas points.

There were a few notable exceptions to the studio rule, among them *The Grapes of Wrath,* shot at various points on Route 66; and *Stagecoach,* made in Monument Valley, north of Gallup, and the Spencer Tracy-Katherine Hep-

There are still signs of life on the remnants of Old Route 66.

burn film *The Sea of Grass*, which was made on the highway. The classic *Gone with the Wind* was made entirely at a studio.

In 1936, the prelude to World War II started with the revolution against the democratic government of Spain by General Francisco Franco, backed by Adolf Hitler and Benito Mussolini, the Italian dictator.

After America entered World War II following the Japanese attack on Pearl Harbor in 1941, civilian traffic on Route 66 slowed to a trickle because of gas rationing and the nation's involvement in the conflict, with many young men in the services and their wives working in arms factories. Military convoys began to travel across the highways with men and machines, taxing Route 66's durability and capacity, built when two lanes were great and traffic was light. When the government established military bases, the wives of servicemen followed and rented motels, bringing more life to small towns which once made their livings from tourists. Getting their first taste of the West at the military bases, many servicemen decided they wanted to live there after being discharged.

When the war ended in 1945 and gas was no longer rationed, the flow of traffic began again with a trek westward by people who wanted to try different kinds of living. With automobiles again available, motorists yearned to enjoy the great American pastime of hitting the open road. California had become a fabled never-never land, thanks to decades of movies, picture postcards, intense "come-visit-us" advertising by boosters, and exuberant letters from friends who had gone ahead, plus the praises of men stationed in the Golden State or other western areas while in the service.

When you leave the interstate and drive on Old Route 66, you get an idea of what travel was like in the 1920s through early 1980s. The Santa Fe Railroad parallels "66" from Texas to California, and while passenger service has been reduced to a single Amtrak in each direction, reminders of the glory days of rails can be seen. Several pretentious Harvey Houses remain even though they are

John Manning Mayo in 1929 posed for this photograph on Bill Williams Avenue, at the time used by Route 66 for traffic in both directions. (Courtesy Hubert A. Clark Jr.)

no longer open. Among those still standing are ones at Winslow and Seligman in Arizona and at Needles and Barstow in California. The one in Williams serves as a depot and souvenir shop for riders of the Grand Canyon Railway. All five provided overnight accommodations as well as meals. A sixth, El Tovar Hotel at the Grand Canyon, still operates.

London-born Fred Harvey (1835-1901) went into the restaurant business after arriving in America as a young man. Depressed by the quality of meals on railroads, he persuaded the Santa Fe Railroad to form a partnership with him to furnish meals for the line's passengers; the legendary Harvey Girls provided charming service and the meals were delicious. Besides other places, the Harvey Houses stretched across portions of northern New Mexico and Arizona parallel to Route 66. Some served food exclusively, while others also provided hotel accommodations

Route 66, four lanes wide at this point, stretches westward from Seligman alongside the Santa Fe Railroad tracks. BELOW: Angel Delgadillo, born in 1927 at Seligman, operates a combination barber shop and Route 66 souvenir store. (Both Photographs by the Author)

for the public or passengers awaiting train connections.

Of interest is the fact that not only trains but buses carried people in substantial numbers during the Old Route 66 era. One line was the Greyhound ("Leave the Driving to Us") and its competitor was Santa Fe Trailways, known as Trailways after the Santa Fe Railroad sold the operation.

It was appropriate that the Harvey organization would build these facilities as they did in New Mexico and Arizona because of the fascinating tourist attractions. Older maps show the settlement of Navajo, very properly named because of the people who live in the area. Once an active trading post, in the 1990s it was little more than a landmark with a giant "open" sign even though little remains there to be open. Between Navajo and the next town, Holbrook, is the road to the Petrified Forest National Park, which was a Na-

A 1962 view of Kingman showed Route 66 entering the city alongside the Santa Fe Railroad.

tional Monument until 1992.

Next is Holbrook, where one can turn onto Old Route 66 with its museum and a very unusual place for lodging: The Wigwam Motel, built in the mid-1930s and still open for visitors. There is a similar motel in Rialto, constructed at approximately the same time. These motels actually follow the architectural lines of a teepee, used by Plains Indians. A wigwam is a similar but less spectacular structure. Just south of Winslow and Holbrook is the Petrified Forest National Park, a 147-square mile preserve and the adjacent Painted Desert, the 150-mile long region of mesas and plateaus with hues of purple, red, and brown rock which defy imitation by an artist. Approximately 20 miles west of Winslow and south of the highway is Meteor Crater, formed 50,000 years ago when a meteor crashed to earth.

Just before Flagstaff is the Twin Arrows Trading Post, aptly marked with two giant arrows rising from the ground. The author always will remember this landmark. In the early 1950s the author and his mother, Mrs. Jessie Person Crump, were travelling westward on Route 66 when approximately one-fourth mile east of the arrows he ran out of gasoline. There was little highway traffic on the highway as he hiked to the settlement. A few minutes later, a woman who also ran out of gas arrived with a motorist who gave her a lift and graciously provided rides back. What a difference time made! Today one would not consider leaving a woman alone in a car, and few people would accept a ride with strangers.

Flagstaff itself is a colorful city, where Old Route 66 takes the name Santa Fe Avenue and stretches from one end of town to the other, following the tracks of the Santa Fe Railroad. Looming in the background is San Francisco Peak, which offers great skiing during winters. Vintage motels and restaurants are mixed with modern ones. San Francisco Street, with its north and south sections divided by Santa Fe Avenue, was the town's original main street, and numerous early-day buildings, most of them in excellent condition, remain. South San Francisco Street leads down to Arizona State University, and along it are coffee shops and cafes reminiscent of those in Berkeley.

Farther west is Williams, named for trapper-preacher Bill Williams and gateway to the Grand Canyon National Park — approximately 65 miles from Route 66. In Williams, Route 66 originally followed Bill Williams Avenue, the city's main street. When traffic increased, it was diverted so that eastbound vehicles used Bill Williams Avenue and westbound ones travelled on Railroad Avenue, a block away. The Grand Canyon is America's most popular national park, and starting in 1903 the Santa Fe Railroad began running passenger service there from its new line that

started in Williams.

The Santa Fe's peak year for carrying passengers by rail to the Canyon was, perhaps not coincidentally, 1927 — the year after which Route 66 was established and made automobile travel easier. Declining rail traffic resulted in the route's closure in 1968. Rail service resumed in 1989 after new orders revitalized the line.

Proud of its heritage, residents of Kingman decorated this tank alongside Route 66. A sign heralds the "66" souvenirs on Andy Devine Avenue in Kingman. (Both Photographs by the Author)

In the 1930s the Bank of America grew into a major American institution. Its branch in Needles was on U.S. Route 66 across from the Santa Fe depot. (Bank of America Archives)

Part of Route 66, which is a main street in Kingman, is named for one of its favorite citizens, the gravel-voiced comedian Andy Devine (1905-1977), who played the driver in the John Wayne movie *Stagecoach* and was a sidekick for Jack Benny on his radio shows. He was born in Flagstaff and reared in Kingman.

Old Route 66 is well preserved between Kingman and Oatman, but as noted above has the same perilous curves that slowed the Oklahoma migrants. Oatman, once a mining settlement, is now a lively ghost town. The city achieved a measure of fame because Clark Gable and Carole Lombard honeymooned thereafter being married in 1939 at Kingman.

Crossing the Colorado River at Topock, Route 66 went into California over a bridge since retired from automotive traffic. Here is Needles, a Santa Fe Railroad center and the stopping place for fuel, food, soft drinks, and overnight accommodations.

The stretch of the highway from Needles to Barstow was an arduous one in "66" days. Continuing to parallel the Santa Fe tracks, the highway went south of where Interstate 40 would be built. Leaving the interstate, drivers today can travel Old Route 66 through Essex, Ludlow, and Newberry, towns that are shadows of their former selves. Here and there are junk yards for automobiles which couldn't quite make it in the desert heat or were involved in wrecks. Here are vintage service stations and motels, seemingly

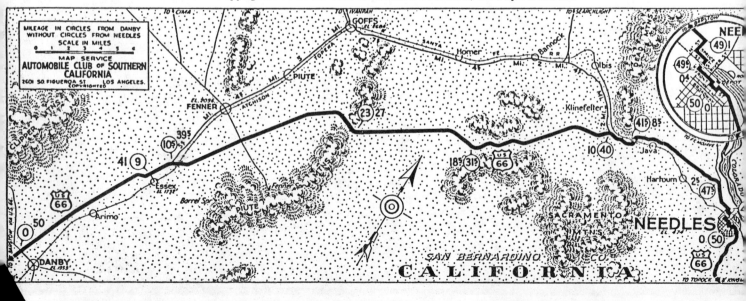

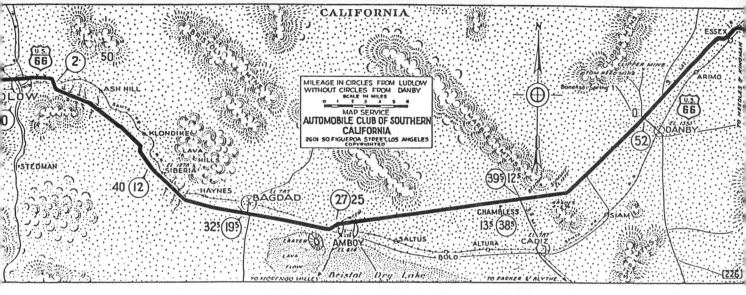

waiting for hordes of tourists to return although in fact few cars go through the area.

Route 66 led on through Daggett and into Barstow via Main Street, an artery which welcomed thousands of travellers through the years and still greets motorists.

The post-World War II surge over Route 66 brought, among others, a young musician and song writer named Bobby Troup with his then-

wife, Cynthia. Inspired, Troup wrote the immortal song, *Get Your Kicks on Route 66*. It was an immediate hit. (See Pages 12 & 13.)

Between Barstow and Victorville, Interstate 40 swings to the east of Old Route 66. The highway, with hills and curves, went through Lenwood, a place that still exists with part of it being moved to the interstate. Route 66 then went to Helendale, which was so small in "66" days that it was barely

An early photograph shows the bridge that carried Route 66 over the Colorado River at Topock. (Lake County, Illinois, Musuem/Curt Teich Postcard Archives)

COLORADO RIVER BRIDGE. TOPOCK. ARIZONA

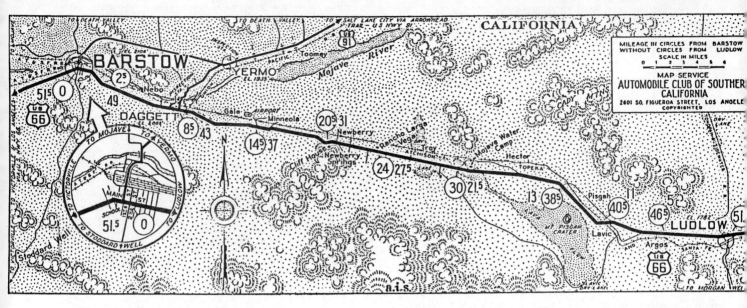

recognizable; it is now a retirement community. Old "66" took travellers onto Main Street in Victorville and then through the forest of Joshua Trees, then unbroken by tract homes. Old Route 66 curved through Cajon Pass, over what has now become multi-laned Interstate 40. Traces of "66" remain and can be reached by exits noting their locations. The highway then leads down to San Bernardino, surrounded by orange groves until the early 1960s when developers downed them to build houses. Highway 66 entered San Bernardino on Mount Vernon Avenue, near where a drive-in restaurant of an unusual type was situated in the early 1950s. It had been the kind of eatery where a car-hop, after receiving a food order, carried the meal to an automobile and then repeated the se-

quence with another customer. The owners, whose names were McDonald, decided they would get more business if they eliminated car service and sold hamburgers through windows. Ray Kroc, in the business of selling food processors, was surprised at the number of milk shake machines that the little restaurant ordered. He visited the establishment and saw a new concept in food service. He bought the restaurant and its concept, and built the chain that became synonymous with fast food.

San Bernardino was more or less a junction from where motorists could take highways to nearby Riverside, also in the Orange Empire, and down to San Diego, Orange County, or Long Beach, where many people from the Midwest or Texas vacationed and eventually settled. When Disneyland opened in the mid-1950s, visitors began leaving Route 66 in San Bernardino to drive directly to the Anaheim area.

Leaving San Bernardino on Fifth Street, Route 66 became Foothill Boulevard as it entered the town of Rialto, a community noted for its acres of orange trees and vineyards. To the right was the Wigwam Village Motel, a twin to the one in Holbrook. The highway continued on through Fontana, which would boom with building of the

When Route 66 reached Barstow, it crossed over the Santa Fe Railroad tracks and offered a view of the Harvey House and depot. The Amtrak train was stopping there in this 1990s photograph. BELOW: Automobiles from wrecks dating back to the 1940s fill this area in Essex on Old Route 66. (Both Photographs by the Author)

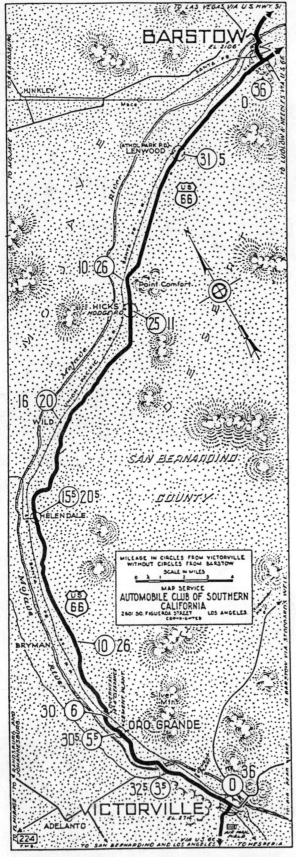

Kaiser Steel mill during World War II. Heading to Los Angeles, the highway went by the picturesque vineyards and wineries of Cugamonga and lush orange grove cities of Ontario, Pomona, Claremont, LaVerne, San Dimas, Azusa, and Monrovia. On clear days, and most days were clear in the pre-smog era that ended in the late 1940s, a magnificent scene was created by the backdrop of the towering San Gabriel Mountains with orange groves in the background. In the winter, the views were even more spectacular when snow on the mountains produced the contrasts of snow and luxuriant fruit-laden orange trees.

On clear days the view is still spectacular, but the trees are gone, with dwellings and stores taking their place.

Route 66 indeed offered captivating attractions over more than two thousand miles all the way, as Bobby Troup put it. For example, the writer in 1972, with his then-wife, Mary, and children, John and Victoria, and mother, Jessie Person Crump, left for a leisurely sightseeing trip from the Los Angeles area to an appointment in New York City. We got an early start, but were slowed while the kids marvelled at the Roy Rogers Museum in Apple Valley (since moved to alongside the Interstate 40 in Victorville). We managed to make it to Kingman despite stops for food and souvenirs, and obtained a motel. While dining, we met a neighbor also heading east, whose rented motor home broke down while travelling over the desert hills. He was marooned until repairs could be made.

We also were slowed, of course, by our Volkswagen camper which overheated and barely made it over hill and dale; on the parts of the highway with just two lanes in "no passing" sections, we pulled over on the shoulder, with some embarrassment because of our speed or lack of it — to permit the faster automobiles to pass. By the time we visited relatives in Texas, the home of

This is the original McDonald's Restaurant on "D" Street north of Base Line Avenue in San Bernardino. The site is noted by an historical marker. BELOW: A 1930s photograph shows San Bernardino's "E" Street looking north from Third.

BD-8—E Street from Third, San Bernardino, California

The 1904 Ford Model B was produced four years after the Automobile Club of Southern California was organized. (Ford Motor Company Archives)

Getting the Kicks on Route 66

The maps in this book originally appeared in the guide *National Old Trails Road and U.S. Highway 66*, published in 1932 by the Automobile Club of Southern California Ltd., and are reproduced with that organization's permission. The maps are treasures when it comes to looking at the way America appeared in the 1930s, at least the Route 66 portion of the nation.

The Automobile of Southern California was the nation's first auto club, being founded in 1900 or three years before similar organizations in other states. In an era before state or federal agencies posted directions or mileages, the Auto Club assisted early motorists by erecting signs to guide the adventuresome.

For the 1932 guide, Auto Club cartographers meticulously charted the locations of even the smallest towns, rivers, creeks, and railroads that long ago changed their names or quit operating.

In making these maps available, Thomas V. McKernan Jr., Club president; Chief Cartographer William R. Scharf, and Jeffery Wilensky, who researched them, provided a service for preserving

Americana for afficianados of history.

Motoring was an adventure in the Route 66 era, and from its start the Automobile Club helped make it a pleasant one. It indeed earned its slogan, "A Friend to Motorists Since 1900," and still serves car owners. The modest membership fee provides a variety of services ranging from emergency road service to assistance in world travel reservations. Address: 2601 S. Figueroa Street, Los Angeles, CA 90007.

Even though the organization was California-based, its guide began at the eastern end of the highway. This was because most Americans resided in the Midwest or East, and they would journey westward for sightseeing and new homes.

Route 66 also was known as The Road to California. When the highway was born, the census gave Los Angeles a population of 936,455 people and California 3.4 million. By the time interstate ended Route 66 in 1984, Los Angeles had 3 million residents and the Golden State was home to 26.9 million.

Southern California's beach cities offered big attractions for visitors from the East, as they still do. Tourists, and locals, too, enjoyed the Long Beach Salt Water Plunge, which was filled with filtered and warm water from the Pacific. It was demolished in the late twentieth century.

Getting More Kicks on Route 66

Route 66 Magazine, P.O. Box 66, Laughlin, Nevada 89028, publishes fascinating articles of Route 66 places and people. Aficionados of Route 66 will find it well worth the price of a subscription.

Several independent Route 66 associations and information centers promote the attractions of the historic highway and variously offer publications, local information, and memberships. Here, subject to changes, is a partial list of them:

Route 66 Association of Illinois, P.O. Box 8262, Rolling Meadows, Illinois 60008.
Missouri Route 66 Association, P.O. Box 8117, Saint Louis, Missouri.
Kansas Route 66 Association, P.O. Box 169, Riverton, Kansas 66770.
Oklahoma Route 66 Association, 901 Marvel Avenue, Chandler, Oklahoma 74834.
Route 66 World Association, Casa Grande Hotel, 204 North Main, Elk City, Oklahoma 73644.
Route 66 Museum, 2229 Gary Boulevard, Clinton, Oklahoma 73601.
Old Route 66 Association of Texas, P.O. Box 66, McLean, Texas 79057.
New Mexico Route 66 Association, 1405 San Carlos, No. 6, Albuquerque, New Mexico 81704.
Historic Route 66 Association of Arizona, P.O. Box 66, Kingman, Arizona 86402.
Old Route 66 Visitor Center, Milepost 81, Highway 66 Hackberry, Arizona 86411.
Route 66 Territory Museum, 8916-C Foothill Boulevard, Rancho Cucamonga, California 91730
California Route 66 Museum, 16849 "D: Street, Victorville, California 92392.
California Route 66 Association, 2117 Foothill Boulevard, No. 66, LaVerne, California 91750.

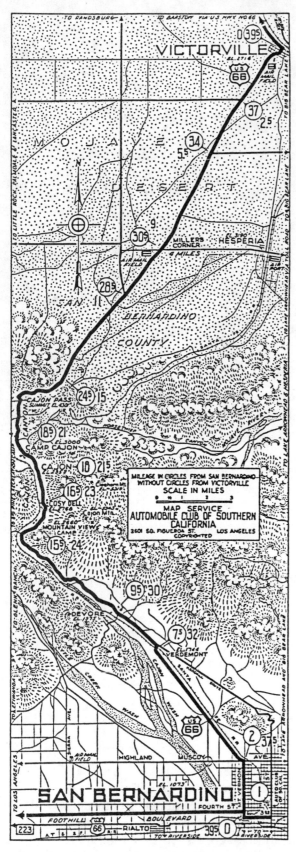

Will Rogers in Claremore, the Mississippi River at Saint Louis, and countless tourist "traps," each of them enjoyable, we determined we had run out of time. There were too many attractions that made us stop. We loved, however, every stop. Still wanting to see more of the country, although from a window, we boarded a train for the balance of the journey.

Route 66 unfolded magnificent sights as it continued to Los Angeles and then its terminus at Santa Monica. The communities along the base of the mountains after leaving San Bernardino comprised southern California's beautiful Orange Empire, aptly named for the waxy green trees which stretched for miles. This was the place where the promises made in tourist advertising came true. Travellers a few minutes before were in the desert, and now in a 15-minute drive could motor from the groves to the snow, and then down for the contrast of wading in the Pacific Ocean.

Appreciative of the area, many southern Californians took pleasure drives on Saturdays or Sundays to enjoy the orange trees, vineyards, wineries, and quaint old towns.

Southern California's famous orange groves were virtually eliminated in the 1960s when developers acquired them for housing tracts, and the vineyards met the same fate in the decades that followed. The name Orange Empire no longer appropriate, the region was thereafter called the Inland Empire.

Route 66 continued through the foothill towns of Duarte, Monrovia, Alhambra, and Arcadia, and in Pasadena turned onto Colorado Boulevard, the city's business district and the street on which the Tournament of Roses parade is held on New Year's Day.

In 1947 television, available in 1936 in Great Britain, began a familiar part of the American scene even though all reception was in black and white. The initial TV sets listed for $400 to $600 and were for models with screens 10 or 12 inches

A 1920s view from Mount Lowe, just above Pasadena, shows that one could see clearly Catalina Island 40 miles away, with Los Angeles, Santa Monica, adjacent cities, and then undeveloped farmlands in the foreground.

wide. This was a substantial price at a time when only a few workers earned $600 a *month*. Seven-inch sets commanded $200 to $300. Bars and clubs installed television sets as a drawing card for patrons; much of the programming featured wrestling and early sound movies, including the serials shown years before at children's matinees. Offerings later expanded to variety shows featuring artists such as Lucille Ball, Sid Caesar, Milton Berle, and entertainers from radio such as Jack Benny and George Burns and Gracie Allen.

TV soon was luring crowds by the thousands from motion picture theater audiences. The studios fought back. Heretofore pictures were shown in what essentially was a square screen. In 1954, Twentieth Century-Fox studios released *The Robe*, a film that alone would have been a spectacle but became more fascinating because it used a process called CinemaScope which elongated the screen. That system ended "square" movie screens, and all pictures soon were made with that technology or variations of it.

From Colorado Boulevard, Route 66 initially turned left on Los Robles Avenue to Huntington Drive. Here for a short time the highway travelled adjacent to the right-of-way of the Pacific Electric

The motion picture greats of bygone days appear to be looking at the spectators in this mural on the west side of Wilcox Avenue just south of Hollywood Boulevard. (Photograph by the Author)

Railroad, which with more than 1,200 miles of track once was the largest interurban system in America. Oddly, the P. E. system hit its peak of operations in 1926, the year that Route 66 was established and more people took to automobiles. From Huntington Drive, the highway travelled to Los Angeles by way of North Broadway. When the Arroyo Seco Parkway opened, one of America's first freeways, Route 66 went onto it.

The building of the interstates had the effect of a bomb dropping on the Route 66 communities, except for the large cities that did not need tourists to survive. When words of the super-highways developed, communities and organizations lobbied against the changes. They argued pitifully for the interstate to forget bypassing *our* town, but obviously the decision-makers in Washington, D.C., and the state capitals would not change

plans, although they told constituents that they were "sorry." Realizing what was ahead, some motel and restaurant owners moved to other cities or different businesses. Some remained because of family and sentimental times.

The actual "bomb" that would eventually wreck many towns began in 1944 with legislation designed to bring about new highway systems for America. The Highway Revenue Act of 1956 produced the Highway Trust Fund with pay-as-you-go financing. The federal government would provide 90 percent of the costs and the balance would come from individual states. The actual construction involved various sections, one section at a time of interstate mileage paralleling Route 66. As crews completed portions of the new highway, sections of the towns bypassed seemed deserted. New and larger motels and truck/automobile gasoline stations were erected at interstate junctions. Automobiles and trucks raced pass Old Route 66 on the new giant slab up to 10 miles away.

The double-building Rosslyn Hotel, at Fifth and Main Streets which in the 1920s to 1940s was in the downtown area of Los Angeles. Meals in the 1930s cost less than a dollar in a dining room with tablecloths and cloth napkins.

Unlike the massive freeway structures, Route 66 varied over the years in the Los Angeles area streets it covered. In the early days it went on Sunset Boulevard. Travelling west on Sunset, one came to the Twentieth Century-Fox Studios on the southwest corner of Vermont Street; a shopping center now occupies the site, but at the rear are the massive buildings of the remaining sound stages. A few blocks farther west, again on the left side of Sunset, are the studios of KTLA-TV Channel 5 and KMPC Radio. These buildings originally comprised the Warner Brothers-First National Studios, which produced the first sound motion picture, *The Jazz Singer*.

A few blocks north of Sunset is Hollywood Boulevard, over which many visitors to southern California drove because of its fame. A philosopher once said that Hollywood was not a place but a state of mind, and this is probably very true. Yet, Hollywood Boulevard from the 1920s through the early 1960s exuded the romance and sparkle of motion pictures. The fact that the studios in those days made a higher percentage of the pictures on their sound stages and back lots gave employment to both actors and technicians, many of whom resided in the nearby apartment buildings and residences. There were many shops stocked with stylish clothing, and here or there were stores selling items directly connected to the studios and their employees. Strolling along the boulevard on almost any day, one could see familiar faces from the screen, and

 is the photograph with caption.

51   West Adams Street, Los Angeles, Calif.

Los Angeles' Adams Street went through a prime residential area in the 1920s and 1930s. It was renamed to honor the great American civil rights leader, Martin Luther King Jr.

if the personalities observed one staring, he or she would smile and speak. There are many "street" people on the sidewalks today that sometimes seem "lost," and many hotels and business buildings are decaying because of age and earthquakes. Despite this, one can in a way relive the old era on Hollywood Boulevard and along Vine Street by examining the "stars" imbedded in the cement. These names on the plaques commemorate the celebrities of the silent days as well as those of the sound era. One feels a bit of a thrill in knowing that the famous and near-famous probably stood on the sidewalk the day their "star" was placed there.

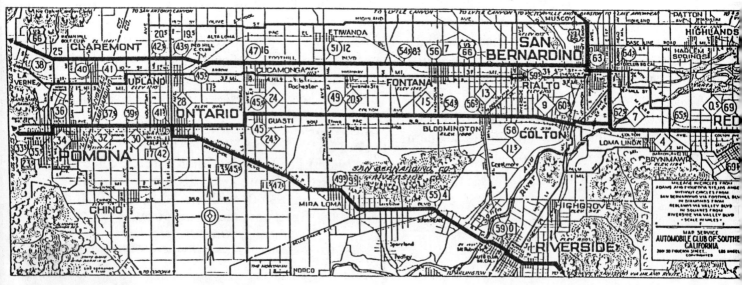

Oranges and Snow in
California.

The scene of the sunny orange groves nestling beneath the mountains by Route 66 became a
southern California trademark that vanished with the housing boom of the 1950s and 1960s.

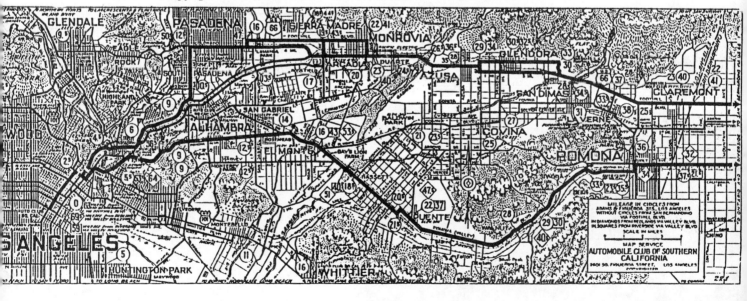

U. S. Highway 66

1B-H2162

41:—Spring Street, looking North from Seventh, Los Angeles, Cal.

When the Arroyo Seco (Spanish for "Dry Wash") Parkway between Los Angeles and Pasadena was completed as one of America's first freeways, Route 66 turned on it. This is a 1940s photograph. LEFT: A 1920s photograph shows Spring Street at Sixth, for years Los Angeles' financial district.

In the Hollywood-Vine area there are several attractive and realistic murals which depict actors and actresses from different eras seated or talking together. One particularly dramatic mural is on the west side of Wilcox Avenue between Hollywood and Sunset Boulevards. Stars of several eras are seated together in a theater, and they appear to be looking at passers-by on the sidewalk.

After years of building the new interstates and bypassing Route 66, the time came for ceremonies saluting its closing. The place was Williams, a town which had prospered over the years with its friendly motels, restaurants, automobile servicing facilities, and highway to the Grand Canyon. The day for celebrating the closing of Route 66 and the opening of Interstate 40 was Saturday, October 13, 1984.

Just down the coast from Santa Monica and the terminus of Route 66 are several seashore towns. ABOVE: Long Beach had its Rainbow Pier and a panorama past orange groves to the mountains. BELOW: Here is the Hermosa Beach Hotel which in the early 1940s advertised rooms for $12 a week.

CATALINA ISLAND

Surf
AUTO HOTE
SANTA MONICA,

Route 66 ended in Santa Monica at the Pacific Ocean, where tourists could stop at this seaside motel.

Attending the ceremony were hundreds of aficionados of the old route, representatives of the news media, and, appropriately, Bobby Troup.

He sang his great composition, *Get Your Kicks on Route 66*, and there probably wasn't a dry eye in the crowd.

There were no official temperature readings because it was Saturday, but Williams historian Teri Cleeland reports that a legend has it that the high was *66* and the low was *40*.

From Sunset Boulevard in Hollywood, Route 66 turned onto Santa Monica Boulevard, travelling over that artery until reaching Santa Monica. Once there, it proceeded to the Pacific at Ocean Avenue.

And that was the end.

END OF ROAD

176